CADETS AND THE WAR, 1939 - 1945

Dr Larry J. Collins served as a cadet with the A.C.F. before enlisting as a Junior Leader with the Royal Signals in 1957. He left the Army in 1966 to train as a teacher of physical education and history at Madeley College where he graduated with a B.Ed. In 1974, after gaining an M.A. from Leeds University, he lectured at Worcester College of Higher Education. A change of career occurred in 1980 when he entered the theatrical profession. A return to academia resulted in a Ph.D. in theatre history being completed in 1994. The military connection was resumed in 1986 when he was commissioned into the R.A.F.V.R. (T) where he served with the A.T.C. in Essex. In 1991, on moving to Hertfordshire, he transferred to the A.C.F., and whilst there also served with the C.C.F. A further move in 1994 meant a transfer to Somerset A.C.F. and in 1996 to Shropshire, where he resides today. In 2004 he became the Deputy Commandant of Cheshire A.C.F.

Larry J. Collins still writes and also teaches part-time. In June 2000 he was awarded the MBE for services to the Army Cadet Force.

Other publications:

Theatre at War, 1914 - 18 [1998 Macmillan] hardback
CADETS - The Impact of War on the Cadet Movement [2001 Jade Publishing Ltd.] paperback
Theatre at War, 1914 - 18 [2004 Jade Publishing Ltd.] revised edition in paperback

CADETS
and the
WAR
1939-1945

L J COLLINS

◇JADE◇

Jade Publishing Limited,

5, Leefields Close, Uppermill, Oldham, Lancashire, OL3 6LA.

This first impression published in paperback by Jade Publishing Limited 2005.

ISBN 1 900734 39 7 Cadets and the War, 1939–1945. (Pbk).

Printed in Great Britain

Typeset by
Jade Publishing Limited, Oldham, Lancashire.

British Library Cataloguing in Publication Data
Collins, L.J., 1942–
 Cadets and the War, 1939–1945 – New Ed.
Includes bibliography and index.
 1. World War, 1939–45 – Cadets and the war
I. Title
940.4'8

ISBN 1–900734–39–7

ABBREVIATIONS

A.C.F.	Army Cadet Force
A.D.C.C.	Air Defence Cadet Corps
A.P.T.C.	Army Physical Training Corps
A.R.P.	Air Raid Precautions
A.T.C.	Air Training Corps
A.T.S.	Auxiliary Territorial Service
B.E.M.	British Empire Medal
C.C.F.	Combined Cadet Force
C.P.O.	Chief Petty Officer
D.S.O.	Distinguished Service Order
G.N.T.C.	Girls' Nautical Training Corps
G.M.	George Medal
G.T.C.	Girls' Training Corps
H.G.	Home Guard
H.M.S.	His Majesty's Ship
H.R.H.	Her Royal Highness
J.T.C.	Junior Training Corps
L.D.V.	Local Defence Volunteers
M.P.	Member of Parliament
N.A.T.C.G.	National Association of Training Corps for Girls
N.C.O.	Non-Commissioned Officer
N.L.S.C.C.	Navy League Sea Cadet Corps
P.T.	Physical Training
R.A.F.	Royal Air Force
R.A.S.C.	Royal Army Service Corps
R.E.M.E.	Royal Electrical and Mechanical Engineers
R.O.C.	Royal Observer Corps
S.C.C.	Sea Cadet Corps
T.A.	Territorial Army
T.S.	Training Ship
U.T.P.	Upper Thames Patrol
W.A.A.F.	Women's Auxiliary Air Force
W.J.A.C.	Women's Junior Air Corps
W.R.N.S.	Women's Royal Naval Service

CONTENTS

Cover by: Baxter-Cox Design

ACKNOWLEDGEMENTS

My acknowledgements are many. Pictorial evidence was viewed and some reproduced thanks to the Department of Photographs at the Imperial War Museum, Royal Air Force Museum and courtesy of Brenda Layne MBE, Director of the Girls' Venture Corps Air Cadets. Stills were taken with permission from Greenpark Production Ltd. Newspaper and magazine photographs are reproduced courtesy of The Westmorland Gazette and Hertfordshire Pictorial, and the Sea Cadet Corps, Army Cadet Force and Air Training Corps headquarters. Thanks also to Sedbergh, Rugby, and Birkenhead School and Stonyhurst College.

I am indebted to Les Berks for his expertise when compiling the myriad of photographs of different standards. Thanks too to Pamela Daniels for her proof-reading skills, and to Brian Prescott of Jade Publishing Ltd for his editorial advice. Mention must be made of the encouragement given by Brigadier Ian McGill, CBE, General Secretary A.C.F.A., and the financial generosity of the Army Cadet Force Association, without whose help this book would not have been published.

In addition, I am indebted to numerous individuals, too many to mention personally, who gave freely of their time and effort. Individual recognition for photographs is given at the end of each chapter. Especial thanks go to Major General His Grace the Duke of Westminster, Assistant Chief of the Defence Staff (Reserves and Cadets) for contributing the Foreword.

Larry J. Collins
Shropshire,
September, 2005.

FOREWORD

by

Major General The Duke of Westminster, KG, OBE, TD, DL
Assistant Chief of Defence Staff (Reserves and Cadets)

Sixty years have passed since the end of the Second World War and ex-servicemen and women justifiably look back with pride at what they achieved. But what about the Cadet Movement, what did the cadets do during the years 1939 to 1945?

With the aid of many hitherto unpublished photographs and an informative text the author explains the effect the Second World War had on the Cadet Movement. It makes fascinating reading and importantly it shows how many of the country's youth contributed to the war effort.

Throughout the history of the Cadet Movement there have been two inter-linked strands. One, which during the time of war comes to the fore, is to provide pre-service military training. The second concerns citizenship training. The latter was not forgotten during the Second World War with cadets raising money for Government-sponsored schemes, sending parcels to the troops, raising working parties to help out at military bases, and providing marching bands for local war related functions.

In 1940 Ernest Bevin, then Minister of National Service, instituted a system of voluntary national service for all youths aged sixteen and over. With most adults being pre-occupied with the war the Government saw the Youth Service, and in particular the uniformed youth organisations as providing guidance, disciple and challenges needed for the post-school development of young people in war time.

This Government, through public encouragement, increased monetary grants, and the demand for a girls' cadet organisation to be formed, greatly aided the expansion of the Cadet Movement.

The main motivation for the phenomenal increase in cadet membership was, however, the desire of the young to 'do their bit for the war effort' — to serve their country. The immediate expansion of the Air Training Corps was a result of the demands of the RAF following the Battle of Britain. Within two years there was a tenfold increase in membership of the entire Cadet Movement. By 1942 the number of young males in the Junior Training Corps, Sea Cadet Corps, Army Cadet Force and the Air Training Corps exceeded half a million. The Cadet Movement provided over 80,000 pre-trained young men for service in the Armed Forces each year of the war.

The War Office, Admiralty and the Air Ministry took a more direct responsibility for the training of the cadets. A new Army based inter-service physical training syllabus was constructed and each Service expanded the technical training element of its programmes. The Navy, for example, started the *Bounty* scheme specifically for the training of signallers, most of whom were from the Sea Cadet Corps. Training manuals were re-written and where possible cadets were involved in realistic military exercises.

Many cadet officers were dual-hatted, in addition being either members of the Civil Defence or the Home Guard. The latter especially had a close relationship with the cadets, particularly the Junior Training Corps (forerunner of the CCF) and the Army Cadet Force. Cadets assisted the ARP and the Royal Observer Corps. In London, as in other parts of the UK, units of cadets were specifically trained to act as messengers in the event of an invasion.

The age of enrolment for a cadet was fourteen which was the age at which most of them left school. The physical and technical training the cadets received could also, as pointed out by the author, be seen as a form of extended education. The changes indicate how the Cadet Movement developed and continued to contribute to the training of young citizens.

By writing this book Lieutenant Colonel Larry Collins, a historian and serving cadet officer, has made a valuable contribution to the history of the Cadet Movement, and alerted readers to the invaluable part the cadets of yesteryear played during the Second World War.

INTRODUCTION

CAME THE HOUR, SO CAME THE YOUTH

The book deals with a little-known facet of Britain at war, building a collection of images to give an insight into the cadets' experiences; showing how they were trained and how the different cadet organisations responded, collectively and individually, to what happened during the Second World War.

Fig 1. Cadets from the Sea Cadet Corps, Army Cadet Force and Air Training Corps.

The photographs, restored to a viewable condition, are drawn from a multitude of sources. Some are reproductions from the cadet journals of the day which, because of wartime conditions were produced on inferior paper, making reproduction difficult at times. A few of the pictures have been secured from school archives and some from private sources. A number of excellent photographs were produced under the auspices of the Ministry of Information and these are reproduced thanks to the photographic archivists at the Imperial War Museum and the R.A.F. Museum Hendon. Alas, because of the security restriction imposed at the time, the information accompanying the photographs was minimal. Others are photographic stills extracted from propagandist wartime films for cadet recruitment. The act of transferring the images from 8mm film to video and then to photographs means that sometimes the definition is not all that may be desired, but they are nonetheless worth viewing and help to provide a more informative picture. Included, also, are some pertinent line drawings.

The participation of youth is portrayed in various categories, which is explicit in the chapter titles. Where possible, the information is dealt with on an inter-services basis as the contribution is viewed as a combined effort. Sections dealing solely with the activities of the Army, Navy and Air Cadets or the National Girls' Training Corps, are included where no alternative is possible.

Cadets and the War, 1939–1945

The Cadet Movement consisted of two factions: the Junior Training Corps (later the Combined Cadet Force) which were the school-based contingents, and the town-based units of the Sea Cadet Corps, Army Cadet Force and the Air Training Corps. The Cadet Movement was single-sex, being for boys only. These organisations came directly under the command of the respective military authorities, namely the Admiralty, the War Office and the Air Ministry.

Additional, uniformed, quasi-military organisations for girls, under the umbrella term "National Girls' Training Corps" were begun in 1942, they were: the Girls' Training Corps, Girls' Naval Training Corps and the Women's Junior Air Corps – all governed by the Ministry of Education and not, as in the case of the boys, the Armed Services. Although these youth organisations were separate, they shared similar objectives and often worked together. It is because of this separateness that a chapter is dedicated wholly to the contribution of the Girls' organisations.

The book, through its pictures and accompanying text is a testament to the contribution made by a large, hitherto unsung, section of youth in Britain in a time of national need and trauma, in what has been referred to as "Britain's darkest and finest hour" – the Second World War.

ILLUSTRATION

Fig 1.   Representatives of the three cadet organisations.
The Story of The Air Training Corps, published by The Air League of the British Empire, 1946

CHAPTER ONE

RECRUITMENT AND EXPANSION

In September 1938 the Prime Minister, Neville Chamberlain, keen to avoid a second World War had negotiated a peace deal with the German Chancellor, Adolf Hitler. A year later, however, as a result of Hitler's invasion of Poland, Britain and France declared war on Germany.

The effect on most people was immediate. The images of the First World War of only twenty years before were still clear in the minds of many, and the fear of aerial bombardment as developed by the Germans during the recent Spanish Civil War, provoked a large evacuation of children from the major cities in Britain to the countryside. The evacuation of teenagers was to have a great effect on the expansion of the Cadet Movement.

Fig 1. Evacuees leaving the South-East of England on their way to a safer area, c.1941. Many of them would join the Cadet Movement when they reached the age of 14.

A boy's desire to enlist in a military organisation depended on a combination of powerful factors that were to do with imperialism and psychology, underpinned by the determined efforts of military and government leaders and the power of the youth culture. 'Patriotism and militarism was positively encouraged both in the written word and in diagrammatic form, as the iconography on school walls showed'.[1] There were illustrated wall charts depicting Nelson's victory at Trafalgar and Wellington's at Waterloo. Those who were at school in the 1950s may still remember the large wall map with its predominantly red shading, which showed the vast extent of the British Empire, and many of the boys' heroic historical figures would have been military men. Also, in the public schools those ex-pupils who were decorated for their military feats in past conflicts were remembered with their names etched in stone or on wood, and in some cases their portraits hung in halls and dining rooms.

Cadets and the War, 1939–1945

It was the written word and the cinema that provided popular culture during the war as television was still in its infancy with only a few hundred sets in the London area able to receive signals. The most influential of the writers, when it came to stimulating recruitment, was undoubtedly W. E. Johns, the creator of the fictitious air ace, Biggles. Captain W. E. Johns, former First World War pilot, according to the compiler of *The Who's Who of Children's Literature*, 'did more for service [and cadet] recruiting than a million posters'.[2] The war provided the author with a wide scope for his writings. This is evident in a number of his wartime titles, which include: *Biggles Goes to War* [1938], *Biggles Secret Agent* [1940], and *Biggles defies the Swastika* [1941]. Johns was also a regular contributor to the *Air Training Corps Gazette*. In response to popular demand and with prompting from the Air Ministry, Johns produced a female counterpart to Biggles, namely Worrals of the W.A.A.F.

The War Office noted the effect that the Biggles books were having on A.T.C. and R.A.F. recruiting, and asked Johns to produce a soldier hero. The result was the appearance of a commando named Lorrington King, known as 'Gimlet'. Gimlet was not Biggles in khaki; his was a totally different character, less gentlemanly, much more aggressive.

The 1930s saw a plethora of entertainingly propagandist films from Hollywood where British Imperialist history was glamorised on celluloid. During the war the British Film industry produced many classic black and white propagandist films such as *In Which We Serve*, *We Dive at Dawn*, *Went the Day Well?*, *The Way Ahead*, and *Target for Tonight*, which are still popular today. In addition there were short films made by leading companies specifically in aid of cadet recruitment. For the Sea Cadets there was *Sea Cadets* or *Nursery of the Navy* and *Wings of the Navy*. For the Army Cadets there was *Prelude to Service*. For the Air Cadets, *Venture Adventure* and *Won't You Join Us?*, and a tri-service film, *Three Cadets*. All were produced between 1942 and 1944.

The drive for cadet recruitment was not reliant on history, fictional military heroes, peer pressure, or a young person's sense of patriotism. The Government gave the Cadet Movement a helping hand in the recruitment of cadets, its aim being social rather than militaristic, although the Armed Services were quick to acknowledge and make use of any assistance with recruiting future members.

The Government was concerned about the lack of welfare and the increasingly disruptive behaviour of some youths. There was no doubt that the growth in juvenile crime in the country towns was due in part to the influx of 'street-wise' evacuees from the major cities. The problem was made worse because of the lack of parental supervision due to the demands of war, with fathers away in the forces and mothers working shifts in the factories.

In an effort to tackle the problem the Government established the National Advisory Youth Council – the forerunner of today's Youth Service which, in co-operation with the Board of Education, issued a directive enjoining local councils to create more boys' clubs, youth centres and to expand training centres for youth, and this included the cadet organisations, now referred to as the Pre-Service Cadet Movement.

In 1941 the Government recommended the registration of all young persons between the ages of 16 and 17 for national service. The youths attending for interviews were advised – they could not be compelled – to join a youth organisation. Not surprisingly, given the wartime needs, many opted for the uniformed, military-orientated cadet organisations. Primarily though, the aim was dependent on a social rather than a military need.

Fig 2. There was an initial shortage of weapons so A.T.C. cadets of the Manchester Wing learnt arms drill with dummy rifles weighted with lead.

Fig 3. Recruiting for the A.T.C. at the Metropole Cinema, Victoria in London, 1941.

At the outbreak of war in 1939 the Sea Cadet Corps had 100 units with 9,000 cadets. The S.C.C. catered for boys only, as did all the cadet organisations at that time. Owing to demand, the age of enrolment was lowered to 14 for all three Services. Following negotiations with the Admiralty the number of units increased to 250 and the Sea Cadet Corps membership increased to 25,000 by 1940. It was not uncommon for a sea cadet unit to have over 150 members. By 1944 the number of sea cadet units had more than doubled to 340 and membership had risen to 50,000.

In 183 of the mainly public schools, the Junior Training Corps provided training for 30,000 cadets. Additionally, other schools were affiliated, not to the J.T.C. but to the Army Cadet Force. The vast majority of Army Cadet Force units were, however, based in towns and were open to any boy who wished to join. The rise in membership of the A.C.F. was phenomenal, and by 1942 topped 200,000. Over eighty per cent of the 1,800 A.C.F. detachments were formed during the Second World War.

Recruitment to the Army Cadet Force was for a time directly affected by the formation of the Air Training Corps. The Air Defence Cadet Corps, the forerunner of the A.T.C., was deemed to be too small and inadequate for the task of training future R.A.F. personnel and a new organisation, the Air Training Corps, was formed in 1941. In order to foster the growth of this new Corps, recruitment to the Army Cadets was suspended for six months.

The A.T.C. had no problem in recruiting members as it had a distinct advantage over the other two Arms. Following the Battle of Britain and victory on 'home soil', the R.A.F. was

3

Fig 4. Their first parade at a Sea Cadet Corps training centre.

seen as the most glamorous of the Services. The flyers, and fighter pilots in particular, became known as the 'Knights of the Air', with the 'flying ACE' acquiring the status of a modern sports star. The R.A.F. being aware of this, placed publicity photos of their heroes in the *Air Cadet Gazette*, complete with names and decorations, in order to encourage recruitment. All of this was to the advantage of the A.T.C. and helped in the drive for recruits. Not surprisingly the growth in squadrons and number of cadets was very impressive. By 1944 the number of units totalled 1,700.

In May 1941, General Lord Bridgeman became the Director General of the Home Guard, which was to the advantage of the Army Cadet Force. Although the A.C.F. was only a small part of the Director's responsibility, the effects were felt immediately. In that month, authority was given for a free issue of basic uniform and equipment to the A.C.F. In the same year the Air Training Corps was formed. So to encourage youths to join the organisation and to foster a feeling of belonging to the R.A.F., the Air Ministry also made sure that their cadets were issued with free uniforms.

Fig 5. RAF Aces publicised in the Air Cadet Gazette in order to aid recruitment.

Fig 6. An ACF Cadet Sergeant acts as quartermaster.

A year later, in 1942, the Admiralty took charge of the Sea Cadet Corps training. The initial discernible advantage of this take-over by the Admiralty was, as with the Army and Air Cadets, the provision of free uniforms for its members. Each cadet aged 14 to 17 was issued with *'Cap, Jumper, Trousers, Collar, Flannel and Jersey, Silk and Lanyard, Great Coat or Oilskin'*.

Imprinted on the Sea Cadet hat band were the initials "N.L.S.C.C". (Navy League Sea Cadet Corps). Some sea cadets made attempts to erase the first two letters in the belief that the three remaining letters made the cap look more 'naval' or 'military'. The Army Cadet Force eventually gave up the forage cap in favour of the khaki beret as worn by soldiers.

The equivalent Girls' organisations were not sponsored by the Armed Services but came under the auspices of the Local Education Authorities which did not have access to equipment; hence the girls had to buy their own uniforms.

Fig 7. Recruits in boiler suits being inspected by Air Commodore Chamier CB CMG DSO OBE, Commandant of the A.T.C., prior to their issue with uniforms, 1942.

Fig 8. Girls' Training Corps in Somerset. Remembrance Parade, c.1945.

In the first three years of the A.T.C's existence, 100,000 boys received pre-service R.A.F. training. The Army Cadets were providing 40,000 partially-trained youngsters for the Army

Fig 9. Pontesbury Detachment, Shropshire A.C.F. 1942 with padre and mascot. Half of the unit consisted of evacuees from Liverpool. Like many other cadet units it lasted for the duration and when the evacuees returned home the unit closed. It was resurrected fifty-five years later.

each year. With 220,000 army cadets, about the same number of air cadets, 50,000 sea cadets and a further 30,000 school-based Junior Training Corps, the number of boys in military uniform totalled well over half a million; 80,000 of whom went into the Armed Forces annually, between the years 1940 to 1945. There is no doubt that the Cadet Movement did the Armed Services, and therefore the country, a service, by providing young men who understood military ranks and discipline, had a grasp of basic skills and were ready for more advanced military training. In total, between 1940 and 1945, nearly half a million cadets went on to serve their country, many of whom were decorated for their service. There is no telling how many soon attained, as a result of their pre-service cadet training, a position of command.

The spirit of the time and the eagerness of boys to contribute to the war effort can best be summed-up in the words of an ex-cadet in the *Hayes Gazette*. It reads:

> *They were eager to do their bit as Hitler dropped bombs on London,*
> *but too young to enlist and the Cadets was the next best thing.*

CHAPTER 1

Recruitment and Expansion

ILLUSTRATIONS

Fig 1.   Evacuees leaving the South-East on their way to a safer area, c 1941.
Maureen Hill, 'Britain at War', *Daily Mail* 2004

Fig 2.   Manchester Wing ATC training with dummy rifles.
Air Training Corps Gazette, 1942

Fig 3.   Recruiting for the ATC at the Metropole Cinema, Victoria, 1941.
Air Training Corps Gazette, 1942

Fig 4.   First parade at a Sea Cadet Corps training centre.
The Navy – organ of the Navy League, 1941

Fig 5.   RAF Aces publicised in the *Air Cadet Gazette*.
Air Training Corps Gazette, 1944

Fig 6.   ACF Cadet Sergeant acts as quartermaster.
The Official Handbook of the ACFA, 1949

Fig 7.   ATC cadets in boiler suits being inspected by Air Commodore
Chamier prior to their issue with uniforms.
Air Training Corps Gazette, 1942

Fig 8.   GTC cadets on Remembrance Parade, 1945
Miss Joan Pitt. Private collection

Fig 9.   Pontesbury Detachment, Shropshire ACF, 1942
Evelyn Cornfield. *Shropshire Unfolded*, 1999

CHAPTER TWO

GETTING FIT TO SERVE

By 1939 it became obvious to everyone that Britain was facing a crisis, and that boys would sooner or later be enlisted into the Armed Forces to help to defend their country and democracy; and it was equally apparent that the effectiveness of a fighting force is to a large extent dependent on the physical fitness of its personnel, especially the front-line troops.

The Cadet Movement and their trainers were aware of the need to get cadets fit for the rigours of training in the Armed Forces. The physical recreation and games periods hitherto undertaken for fun, became more serious and necessarily functional in nature, and the military authorities stressed that physical training should be an integral part of a cadet's training programme. The need for physical fitness was given greater emphasis following the Army's evacuation from the beaches of Dunkirk. The whole experience was a salutary lesson for the planners and trainers. Brigadier Wand-Tetley, writing in *The Cadet Review*, stated that a much higher standard of physical fitness was demanded from cadets and more strenuous physical training tests were introduced into training units[1]. The Cadets' Physical Efficiency Standards became an adaptation of those set for the Army after Dunkirk.

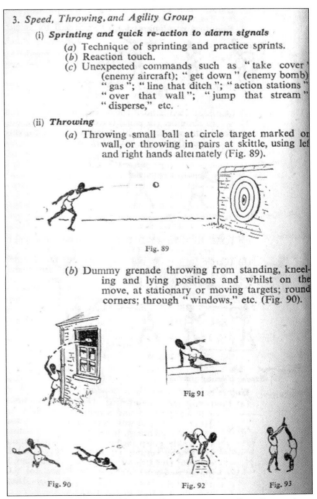

Fig 1. A pre-Service P.T. pamphlet which includes military skills such as grenade throwing exercises, 1943.

Cadets and the War, 1939–1945

In 1943 the War Office produced a pamphlet specifically for the training of army cadets, entitled Pre-Service Physical Training and Recreation for Army Cadets. The pamphlet and the physical tests soon became standardised for all three cadet organisations. A scan through the pamphlet indicates the wartime aims of physical training. Included among the endurance, strength and agility exercises were exercises with a specific military intent – how to throw a grenade, for example.

The Army instituted a Physical Training Leaders course to be run at various Command P.T. schools for cadets over 16, which helped to cater for the wartime need. Those cadets who passed the course would, in effect, be assistant instructors. The Royal Navy and the R.A.F. also began to run similar courses.

The PT courses were held in school holidays and usually lasted for a week to ten days. The Army course held at Western Command in 1943 was for cadets from the school-based Junior Training Corps and the town-based Army Cadet Force units. It included methods of instruction and training on the obstacle course, with tests to assess each cadet's physical efficiency.

Mindful of the lack of equipment and the need to improvise, lessons were provided for instructors and their units in bridge construction using toggle ropes, planks, scaffolding and whatever other materials were to hand.

The tests took into account the differences in age groups and footwear. It was a time of rationing of food and clothes which meant that purchases were dependent upon the required number of coupons. The compilers of the programme therefore set two standards of test: one for boys wearing boots and one for those wearing plimsolls or leather shoes. The tests included the assessment of a boy's strength, agility, endurance – judging by some of the amateurishly constructed obstacles – their courage as well. The stated objective of the cadet physical training courses was twofold: first, the promotion of leadership and secondly, preparation for the Army Cadet War Certificate 'A'. The training included endurance tests, such as covering five miles in one hour and also the organisation of games for fitness and recreation. Use was made of military training camps and barracks where possible, for annual camps. School gymnasiums and playing fields were also utilised for the training of cadets.

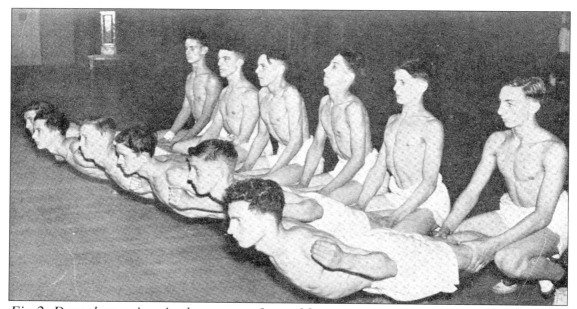

Fig 2. Dorsal exercises in the gym performed by sea cadets.

Fig 3. Army Cadets crossing an improvised toggle rope bridge at camp in 1944.

Fig 4. Cadets doing strengthening exercises with baulks of timber, 1944.

Fig 5. Girls' Venture Corps performing stretching exercises.

The Girls' organisations also included games and physical training in their syllabuses – although judging by some of the pictorial evidence, the girls' physical training was rather more static and included Swedish-style drill movements performed in uniform.

It was pointed out in the Pre-Service Physical Training pamphlet that mechanization had increased rather than decreased the necessity for moral and physical fitness. *"Cadets"*, it was stressed, *"must be trained to walk and run with as little effort as possible over all types of ground and at varying speeds; they must learn to scale or climb ropes, trees, buildings and mountains; to jump or vault natural obstacles skilfully; to lift and carry weights without strain; to throw accurately; to pull or haul their full weight; to swim and to rescue from fire and water"*[2].

In addition to training on the assault course and other military-based physical training, the Sea Cadet Corps included the traditional ship-based hornpipe dance exercises, club swinging exercises and even exercises with the broad-sword cutlass.

Sport, traditionally a part of physical training was included; for the sea cadets this, as expected, incorporated a considerable amount of water-based activity such as swimming,

Fig 6. Dancing the hornpipe on board H.M.S. Indefatigable *at Liverpool where boys aged 13 to 16 were trained, primarily for the Merchant Navy.*

Fig 7. Army Cadets scaling an improvised wall of scaffolding and railway sleepers.

rowing and sailing. Boxing was an integral part of sport in schools and the cadet organisations. From 1944 onwards the latter held their national championships and inter-services boxing matches in the splendour of the Albert Hall in London. These continued until schools banned boxing from their curriculum in the 1960s. Athletics was a favoured summer-time sport and by the end of the war there were inter-services matches in a variety of sports. After the war the Army Cadet Force played cricket against the Air Training Corps on the hallowed square at Lords. The rising cost of travel and accommodation alas, eventually put an end to most inter-service competitions, with the exception of shooting and swimming which continue today at Bisley and the Royal Academy, Sandhurst.

After three years of practical experiment with a large number of cadets in urban and rural districts, the standards were amended and by 1945 the Army had initiated physical training tests which were universally accepted. A Physical Efficiency Preparation pamphlet was produced for use by all three Cadet Services.[3]

Fig 8. Sea Cadets making for the shore.

Fig 9. Playing about in boats.

Fig 10. Army Cadet Force boxing demonstration.

The type of training which appealed to most cadets was that which related directly to their military training. Those responsible for devising the physical training programmes for cadets recommended that such training should be dissimilar to the exercises practised in schools. Pulling a gun, car or truck out of a ditch, rolling a barrel or oil drum up a plane or slope, scaling a wall, climbing a tree or rope were all seen as being more suitable for future servicemen. The Army Cadet Airborne Training Course gave special prominence to these types of activities.

In April 1945 a squad of twenty-six cadets from A.C.F., and J.T.C. units in the Southeast with an officer and two NCO Parachute Regiment instructors, marched through the gates of an airfield near London. On the runway were two Dakota aircraft of the sort used by the R.A.F. to fly British and American air-borne forces on operations. This was an air-experience flight for those cadets attending a special ten-day air-borne course at the London District P.T. School, arranged by the War Office to find out what possibilities existed for air-borne training for cadets.

All those attending the course were required to have passed the Army Cadet War Certificate 'A' and to have taken part in a Command P.T. course. The cadets were therefore senior in age, experience and qualification. Each morning was devoted to *'air-borne P.T., with two A.P.T.C. air-borne instructors in charge'.*[4] The training consisted of jumping from various heights, training on a pulley which hurtled down a wire stretched between two tall trees into a sandpit (commonly known as a 'death-slide') – into which the cadets jumped and rolled. Strengthening exercises figured widely in the programme with forced marches, runs and assault course practice.

Swimming was an important part of the training and the cadets were taught to swim in kit, to improvise aids to cross lakes and rivers, and how to get into and out of floats and dinghies.

14

Fig 11. *Water-borne assault in kit.*

Fig 12. *Survival training in the pool.*

The afternoons and evenings were spent watching demonstrations of various kinds of airborne equipment and tactics; one of the officers was at the Battle of Arnhem and no doubt related his experiences to the cadets. The highlight was a demonstration by an airborne platoon going into action. The cadets also undertook a night exercise.

The intention was produce a pamphlet on modified air-borne training for senior physically-fit cadets, and to arrange for such a course to take place in each Command. Alas there is no evidence of any progress in this form of training, and the ending of the war later that summer, in 1945 meant that there was no further necessity to accelerate the training of cadets.

It would be fair to say that perhaps the most effective and useful service the Cadet Movement rendered to the Armed Forces was the physical preparation of cadets for the rigours of wartime service.

Fig 13. *The first athletics championship after the inauguration of the A.T.C. in 1941.*

Fig 14. *The tests in this 1945 pamphlet set the standard for all three Services.*

15

CHAPTER 2

Becoming fit to serve

ILLUSTRATIONS

Fig 1. Pre-Service Physical Training and Recreation for Army Cadets 1943.
H.M.S.O. The War Office, 1943.

Fig 2. Dorsal exercises in the gym in Ships' Company.
Handbook for S.C.C., The Navy League, c.1945.

Fig 3 Army cadets crossing a toggle rope bridge.
Army Cadet Journal, 1944

Fig 4. Army cadets doing strengthening exercises using baulks of timber.
Army Cadet Journal, 1944

Fig 5. Girls' Venture Corps doing stretching exercises, c.1944.
Courtesy of Girls Venture Corps Air Cadets HQ

Fig 6. Dancing the hornpipe on board HMS Indefatigable.
The Navy – Organ of the Navy League, February 1940

Fig 7. Scaling an improvised wall of scaffolding and railway sleepers.
A.C.F.A. Handbook, 1949

Fig 8. Sea cadets making for the shore.
The Sea Cadet Journal, 1942

Fig 9. Playing about in boats.
The Sea Cadet Journal, 1944

Fig 10. A.C.F. Boxing Demonstration.
Imperial War Museum, H 9758

Fig 11. Water-borne assault in kit.
Still from film the *Three Cadets*, Greenpark Productions 1944

Fig 12. Survival training in the pool.
Still from film the *Three Cadets*, Greenpark Productions 1944

Fig 13. The first A.T.C. athletics championships, 1941.
Golden Jubilee Air Cadets in East Essex Wing, Souvenir Booklet 1991

Fig 14. Physical Efficiency Preparation for Service Cadets.
War Office, 1945

CHAPTER THREE

THE DEMAND FOR TECHNICAL TRAINING

A military force is not composed solely of front-line troops. For every naval gunner, every infantryman and every pilot there were many more serving in a support role as technicians, engineers, mechanics, storemen or clerical workers. The three Services were aware of the need for trainees with a rudimentary technical ability and a level of basic knowledge in core skills such as arithmetic, mathematics, basic science and English.

Practically every serviceman or woman in the Royal Navy and the Royal Air Force had to be proficient in a trade and in the increasingly sophisticated and mechanised Army of the Second World War the same was true for most of the soldiers. According to the Director of Military Training, writing in the 1945 pamphlet, Technical Training in the A.C.F., one soldier in three was required to be a tradesman.[1] At a time when the cadet organisations and cadet training were increasingly coming under the direct control of the War Office, the Admiralty and the Air Ministry, it was inevitable that technical training would figure more often in the cadet programme.

The traditional and necessary skills acquired on drill square, rifle range and assault course would not to be ignored, but they were not sufficient for the would-be serviceman; the Armed Forces required not only the physically fit but mentally capable. Nowhere was this need more obvious than in the field of communications.

Fig 1. Instruction in Morse Code at T.S. Laforey *[Northampton] Sea Cadets c.1943. This unit was better equipped than some and was able to include instruction in wireless telegraphy as part of its cadet training programme.*

Cadets and the War, 1939–1945

As the war gathered momentum it became apparent that the navy was experiencing an acute shortage of visual signallers and wireless ratings. The answer lay in part in the Sea Cadet Corps. The S.C.C. was the only naval youth organisation that was providing training in both semaphore and telegraphy. In response to the increasing demand, the Sea Cadet Corps' governing body, the Navy League, bought and fitted-out an old cargo ship berthed at Worcester in 1940. She was to be used as a base for visual and wireless training, accommodating 40 cadets, and was named *T.S. Bounty*.[2] The Admiralty soon asked for more trained signallers and the S.C.C. headquarters opened a second Signals School at Grenville Hall, Slough.

Fig 2. Advert for the Bounty Scheme in the Sea Cadet Journal, *1943.*

Each month, under the guidance of the Admiralty, the Sea Cadet Corps produced a group of 24 senior cadets trained in signalling up to a specified standard, but this was not nearly enough.

An increase in convoys and the opening of new battlefronts in Europe, later in the war, meant that there was an even greater demand for visual signalman in both the Royal Navy and the Merchant fleets. The training establishments producing Bounty Scheme graduates reacted to the demand and the number of trained signallers trebled from 900 to 2,700 cadets per annum.

Fig 3. Cadet Signaller.

Owing to further expansion the training was re-located to Windermere and finally, in 1943, the visual and semaphore training moved to *H.M.S. Foudroyant* and *H.M.S. Implacable* (formerly the *Duguay Trouin*) in Portsmouth Harbour. These two sailing ships, moored alongside each other, became the HQ afloat of the Sea Cadet Corps.[3]

The War Office stated in *The Cadet Journal*, that '*the Army Cadet Force must not merely turn out Cadets who can shoot, read maps and know the proper use of ground, but also men who can drive and look after lorries and tanks and maintain guns, and who understand radio location and wireless signal apparatus.*'[4] The A.C.F. undertook to meet this demand, and in 1942 a Technical Training Scheme was introduced.

Training for 'Cert. T' as it became known was run concurrently with basic military training, and courses were held at local Evening Institutes and Technical Colleges. The amount of

Fig 4. Nelson's appropriate message hoisted again on H.M.S. Foudroyant *in 1944, "England expects every man to do his duty".*

Fig 5. Leicestershire A.C.F. cadets undergoing signals training in the field, 1944.

technical training available depended on location; the city-based units had greater access to educational facilities. The school-based Junior Training Corps contingents varied in the equipment they had and their training was dependent on the technical expertise of their teachers.

It was some time before radio equipment became generally available but field telephones were more readily obtained. With the deletion of semaphore from the army cadet syllabus, the teaching of Morse Code became more prevalent and lessons in wireless theory and general electricity became part of the Certificate 'T' syllabus.

Where Morse-keys and a Royal Signals or Home Guard signals-trained instructor were available the Morse Code was taught. Some units were fortunate to have access to other signalling equipment such as telephone switchboards.

Training pamphlets included message recording forms devised for training cadets in the taking and passing of verbal and written messages. The initials I.I.M.A.I (Information, Intention, Method, Administration, and Intercommunication) became the format for passing on verbal orders.[5] In all military matters the 24-hour clock is used and this the cadets employed, along with the phonetic alphabet.[6] This training was increasingly useful if a cadet had the opportunity to work as a messenger for the Home Guard, or joined the army as a wireless, telegraph or radio relay operator, with the Royal Corps of Signals; for any future officer the ability to write clear military messages was essential.

The Cert T training was divided into three courses one of which was "Commercial". This dealt with the skills of English, Commercial Arithmetic, Shorthand, Typewriting or Book-keeping.

Each of the Services produced a range of training pamphlets, with the Army Cadet Force and the Air Training Corps printing a pamphlet specifically for the learning of particular writing

20

Fig 6. An A.C.F. cadet N.C.O. taps out the message, the others record what is sent.

skills. With the enormous number of people requiring instruction, the demand was great for coherent officers and senior NCO leaders who could communicate effectively. And their training started as a cadet NCO.

Emphasis was placed on clarity, omission of repetition, precis writing and summary. Interest was added by using examples from military sources; hence, all the précis exercises in the Air Cadets' Handbook of English were taken from Bomber Command reports.[7]

Every effort was made to promote the technical training of cadets. For those who had a particular need, or were enthusiastic, it was possible to purchase an individual Morse Key, to practise at home. The standard for transmission and receiving Morse code for the First Class A.T.C. badge was four words per minute.[8]

Fig 7. A busy cadet telephone operator of the 2nd C/Bn., The East Yorkshire Regiment.

The availability of equipment was variable. It was therefore necessary for cadet units to scrounge or borrow bits of radio kit and batteries, and if necessary to make their own sets of Morse keys. In both the *Sea* and *Air Cadet Journals* there appeared diagrams and instructions on how to construct, for example, an Aldis Lamp. Improvisation and imagination was necessary to provide training in telecommunications.

Underpinning all this technical know-how was a requirement for a basic knowledge of physics, chemistry, and mathematics. The A.T.C. engineering handbooks contained a section dealing with mathematical formulae for this purpose, as did the training pamphlets used by the A.C.F. and the S.C.C.

Fig 8. *Technical training extended cadets' education.*

With the increase in demand for drivers of all types of vehicles there was, of course, an equal need for mechanics. Many boys had an interest in motor mechanics and so there was no shortage of cadets willing to learn about the workings of the Internal Combustion Engine.

When visiting R.A.F. stations, the A.T.C. cadets would be taken on a tour of the different workshops and receive first-hand instruction. Many found a visit to an R.A.F. station quite revealing as they discovered just how much in the way of aircraft maintenance and technical knowledge and skills was required. Some air cadets initially had a 'romantic' view of the R.A.F., and saw it in terms of flying only; a visit and a chat with the ground staff dispelled any misconceptions and made them realise how important and indispensable the aero-mechanic, the welder and the armourer were to the R.A.F.

The Royal Navy started courses for senior S.C.C. cadets which were officially described as *"Petty Officer Training (Mechanic Branch)"*.[9] The courses were divided into two categories: one

Fig 9. *An A.T.C. cadet practises plotting and locating an aircraft's position using radio signals.*

Fig 10 . Instruction for senor A.T.C. Cadets in the use of an Aldis lamp.

was for electrical mechanics, engine-room mechanics, ordnance mechanics, motor mechanics and air fitters; the other for air mechanics.

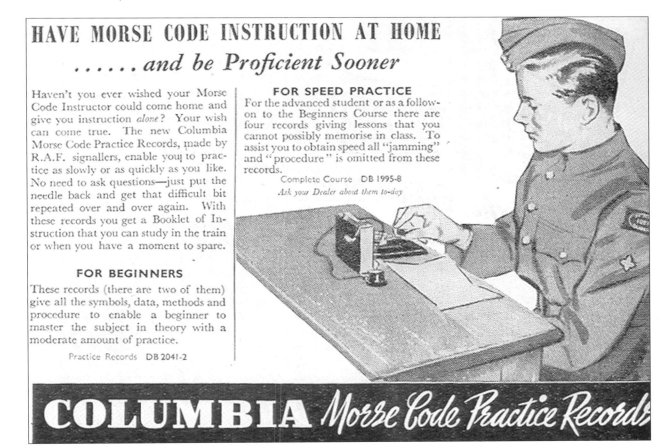

HAVE MORSE CODE INSTRUCTION AT HOME
......and be Proficient Sooner

Haven't you ever wished your Morse Code Instructor could come home and give you instruction *alone*? Your wish can come true. The new Columbia Morse Code Practice Records, made by R.A.F. signallers, enable you to practice as slowly or as quickly as you like. No need to ask questions—just put the needle back and get that difficult bit repeated over and over again. With these records you get a Booklet of Instruction that you can study in the train or when you have a moment to spare.

FOR BEGINNERS

These records (there are two of them) give all the symbols, data, methods and procedure to enable a beginner to master the subject in theory with a moderate amount of practice.

Practice Records DB 2041-2

FOR SPEED PRACTICE

For the advanced student or as a follow-on to the Beginners Course there are four records giving lessons that you cannot possibly memorise in class. To assist you to obtain speed all "jamming" and "procedure" is omitted from these records.

Complete Course DB 1995-8

Ask your Dealer about them to-day

COLUMBIA *Morse Code Practice Records*

Fig 11. Advertisement from Air Cadet Gazette *for Morse code instruction and practice at home.*

Fig 12. A.C.F. cadets learning about electrical circuits.

Whether a cadet wanted to become an officer, a senior NCO or a tradesman in the future; whether he was to be located in an R.A.F. workshop, the engine room of a ship, or working as a R.E.M.E. craftsman on the engine of a tank, he would need to be proficient at his trade, have some knowledge of basic physics, chemistry, electricity, technical drawing and mathematics.

The nearer the experience to the real thing, the better. Later in the war, cadets had the opportunity when visiting an R.A.F. base, a naval dockyard or an army workshop, to get hands-on practical experience.

Fig 13. W.A.A.F. mechanics adjusting spark plugs, watched by A.T.C. cadets.

Fig 14. A.C.F. cadets learning motor mechanics at a local technical college.

During the First World War it was not unusual to have army cadet units belonging to City firms. The practice died out in the 1920s but seemed to have been resurrected by the A.T.C. in London, as indicated by the cadet in Fig. 17 who was from the City of London Insurance squadron.

Fig 15. A.T.C. cadets watching a mechanic at work on a lathe at a Bomber Command station.

Fig 16. A.T.C. cadets at an R.A.F. station examining a Stirling engine.

Fig 17. Cadet of Lloyds and City of London Insurance squadron, doing a spot of welding.

Casualty lists inevitably grew as the war progressed and the need for partially-trained and fit young men increased. By 1943/4 cadet training was able to expand and become more comprehensive, following the Allied Victory in Africa, the invasion of Italy and the stunning success of the D-Day Landings. Pressure on troop training was not so intense at this time and instructors could be spared, which allowed for expansion in cadet training.

More facilities became available and some specialist staff could be assigned to running further short courses for cadets, such as those at the R.A.S.C. Waterborne Training Centre in North Wales. Any course where cadets could get their hands on the actual equipment was popular. They learnt how to strip and re-assemble *Dukws* (pronounced 'ducks') – the famous amphibious assault landing craft used by the army and the commandos – and then launched them into the sea.

Fig 18. Sea Cadets gaining on-board practical experience.

Fig 19. A.C.F. cadets at the Waterborne R.A.S.C. Training Centre. For a day, each cadet was one of the crew of a harbour launch. Two full days were spent at sea.

Making models of ships, aircraft or tanks served several purposes. It was and still is an interesting hobby in itself, but it also had a more practical wartime function in that it helped cadets and servicemen to recognise and identify allied and enemy aircraft; a useful and perhaps even a life-saving skill to have! Training in the recognition of enemy equipment was an integral part of much of the military training and there was no doubt that the ex-cadet, on entry to the Armed Forces, was well ahead of anyone who had not had this training.

The well-equipped A.T.C. squadron that had access to the necessary kits and expert instructors, could take model building a stage further and even build its own glider; and in so doing gain additional knowledge about aircraft construction.

Fig 20. This cadet had found out enough about aircraft recognition to make these models before the details were officially published!

Fig 21. Model making at No. 77 (Cambourne – Redruth) squadron, 1943.

Fig 22. Building a glider; a lesson in technical drawing, woodwork and construction.

Anyone involved in communication and command as an officer or a senior NCO, a signaller or a clerk, would require competence in English. Apart from the Army and Air Cadet booklets dealing with the use of English, the War Office also produced a pamphlet entitled *Message Writing for Cadets* (1945) based on the Signal Message Form AFC2136. Included in the new cadet communication training were lists of some of the abbreviations used by the Services. It was clear that basic numeracy, literacy and an awareness of service jargon were essential for an increasingly technically-orientated military force.

The cadet organisations were quick to produce training pamphlets. New proficiency badges were introduced. The Sea Cadet Corps produced a Cadet Mechanic Badge for their Cadet Petty Officers. The Army saw technical training as another means of turning out trained recruits and the R.A.F. set up an examination system which was controlled by the R.A.F. Central Trade Board. Facilities were provided where possible and detailed scale of provision for technical training became part of the administration. There was an unprecedented liaison with the Local Education Authorities throughout Britain. A boy attending an educational institution for technical training was expected to parade in uniform as it became an integral part of his cadet training programme.[10]

The technical training most cadets received was of benefit to them as individuals, to the Armed Services and later, in civilian life. There is no doubt that for the majority of boys who left school at 14 years of age, membership of a cadet unit could be seen as an extension of their education, albeit with a military bias. This technical training could undoubtedly be viewed as a bonus for the vast majority of the cadets. The syllabus for those cadets remaining at grammar and public schools would no doubt have been influenced by the needs of the military. Subjects such as mathematics and meteorology, for example, must have appeared more relevant, especially for anyone wishing to fly with the Fleet Air Arm or the Royal Air Force.

THE DEMAND FOR TECHNICAL TRAINING

ILLUSTRATIONS

Cadets and the War, 1939–1945

Fig 14.   A.C.F. cadets learning about motor mechanics.
Imperial War Museum. Ref. H 9755.

Fig 15.   A.T.C. cadets watching a mechanic at work on a lathe at a Bomber Command station.
Imperial War Museum. Ref. CH 4743.

Fig16.   A.T.C. cadets at an R.A.F. station examining a Stirling engine.
Air Cadet Gazette, 1944.

Fig 17.   Cadet of Lloyds and City of London Insurance squadron doing a spot of welding.
Air Cadet Gazette, 1944.

Fig 18.   Sea cadets gaining on-board practical experience.
The Sea Cadet Journal, 1942.

Fig 19.   Cadets at the Water-borne R.A.S.C. Training Centre. For a day, each cadet was one of the crew of a harbour launch. Two full days were spent at sea.
Army Cadet Journal, 1944.

Fig 20.   Cadet with models he had made for aircraft recognition.
The Story of the Air Training Corps, The Air League of the British Empire, 1946.

Fig 21.   Model making at No 77 (Cambourne – Redruth) Squadron.
Air Cadet Gazette, 1943.

Fig 22.   Constructing a glider; a lesson in technical drawing, woodwork and construction.
Stills from the film the *Three Cadets* by Greenpark Productions, 1944.

CHAPTER FOUR

TRAINING FOR GIRLS

The Second World War gave women wider scope in the workplace, with conscription for war work in factories, on farms, in the Fire Service and in the Armed Services. This opportunity to help the country in its 'hour of need' was keenly felt by girls.

The desire of girls for greater involvement in the war effort spurred on by the Government's voluntary National Service Register for youths of 16 and over, increased the demand for a uniformed and disciplined cadet organisation for females. The Government, realising that something had to be done, instructed Miss Florence Horsburgh, the Minister for Education, to set up an organisation for girls. As a result the National Association of Training Corps for Girls was formed in 1942.

The N.A.T.C. for Girls encompassed three separate corps: The Girls' Training Corps, Women's Junior Air Corps and the Girls' Nautical Training Corps. The syllabus of the former was general in nature and the Corps became regarded as the female counterpart of the Army Cadet Force. The Women's Junior Air Corps, as the name indicates, specialised in subjects to do with flying. The Girls' Nautical Training Corps' syllabus was the female equivalent of the Sea Cadet Corps.

Fig 1. Representatives of the G.N.T.C., the W.J.A.C. and the G.T.C., c.1942.

Until 1942 the military-orientated youth movements were the preserve of the boys and it is true to say that, for the most part, their organisers were neither geared up for, nor inclined to accept, girls. The newly-formed girls' units naturally approached the existing cadet organisations for assistance. The initial reaction was not always favourable. The S.C.C. Committee sent a memorandum to all of their commanding officers stating that the S.C.C. commission was *"granted exclusively for service with the Sea Cadet Corps"* [1] and that officers who helped the Girls' organisation did so *"in a purely private capacity and not as officers of the S.C.C."* [2] The Air Training Corps was even more condescending saying, *"The young women of Britain want to muscle in on the air training business ... We cannot stop them, we might give them help".* [3] The Army Cadet Force was, however, much more welcoming, stating that *"(we) will be most sympathetic to these new formations, and will extend to them a welcome ... Cadet Units everywhere would be well advised to get into touch with local units of these new formations, and to see how they can co-ordinate their Cadet activities together."* [4]

Any misguided feelings of 'them' and 'us' between the established boys' cadet units and the National Association Training Corps for Girls affiliated cadet units eventually disappeared. It was not uncommon for them to share the same training facilities. At Uxbridge, Middlesex, home of the R.A.F., three strong cadet units were housed, one from the A.T.C., an A.C.F. unit and a Girls' Training Corps contingent. Initially, each unit was

Cadets and the War, 1939–1945

separate but in 1942 they decided to adopt a scheme which involved co-operation and co-ordinated training for the good of all three organisations. A joint training syllabus was prepared. There was also social integration when the G.T.C., opened a canteen, which they managed and the other cadet units raised money to purchase and equip a joint-recreation hut.[5] This was a proposed pattern for future co-operative development. In truth, any integrated development depended to a very large extent on the local commanders; those who were compliant and flexible in approach welcomed the inclusion of girls into the cadet fold, the short-sighted did not.

Fig 2. Women's Junior Air Corps learning practical electrical skills.

Fig 3. Cadets posing with weapons from a bomber, following instruction.

Fig 4. Presentation of W.J.A.C. Standard to the Worthing Unit, c 1942.

The girls' corps, wherever they were located, 'employed' the instructors from the boys' Cadet Movement when they were required to undertake drill, which included forming marching bands. And they, like the boys units, persuaded the Home Guard, the Civil Defence and any other defence organisation to help them train their cadets in useful wartime activities, such fire fighting.

First aid was a pre-requisite of girls' training, as was shorthand, typing and office orderly room procedure; useful skills generally, and particularly helpful for any of the girls who progressed to the Armed Forces. A very large percentage of the clerical and nursing staff of the A.T.S., W.R.E.N.S. and W.A.A.F. were women whose first taste of military-style training came via the cadet G.T.C., the W.J.A.C. or the G.N.T.C.

There was technical training in the form of the study of electricity, care and maintenance of motor transport and for the W.J.A.C., aero engines. Map reading, signalling and Morse Code were common to all three girls' cadet corps; provided they had someone locally to instruct in these subjects.

Aircraft recognition and ·22 calibre rifle shooting was conducted for units which shared their training base with the Army, Sea or Air Cadets that had access to small bore rifle ranges; and in some instances lessons were given by civilian armament specialists on weapons used by Bomber Command gunners.

Drill, physical training – the latter to be taught by qualified women instructors – and organised games were compulsory. The first aid training programme was extended to include

Fig 5. Instruction in map reading for W.J.A.C. cadets, 1942.

general nursing skills and was done under the guidance of the Red Cross, St. John Ambulance Brigade or the A.R.P. ambulance instructors.

An interesting subject practised by the girls was Despatch Carrying. At the G.T.C. unit in Ilminster, Somerset, this was performed on light summer evenings. The objective was to produce a group of reliable, well informed observant messengers. At training meetings

Fig 6. Lady with a Lamp *performed by 228 A.T.C. Squadron and 1165 Unit of the W.J.A.C.*

each cadet was given a verbal message which she had to memorise and at the end of the session the girls were tested. On one occasion a stranger to the district watched their parade for about fifteen minutes before departing. At the end of the evening the cadets, to their surprise, had to produce a written description of the visitor who returned later to hear the descriptions which, on the whole, were remarkably accurate.[6]

This form of training was in keeping with what the Ministry of Information published, for the benefit of security. The Government urged everyone to be vigilant and to report anything that appeared suspicious.

Traditional female subjects such as sewing, cooking and home economics were not forgotten. Cooking tasks were not confined to the normal day-to-day culinary skills – restriction of rations permitting – but also included the setting up of emergency feeding posts. Following bombing raids on the cities and ports, these were essential.

Members of the N.A.T.C.G., had their catering skills tested on those occasions when they rendered great service to the boys' units at summer camps, where there was a shortage of military caterers. They took charge of the cooking, along with the Women's' Voluntary Service (WVS). It was reported in the *Cadet Journal* in 1944, that the W.V.S. and the N.A.T.C. girl cadets, gave help of the *'highest order in many areas, grappling indefatigably with the "unknown quantities" of Army rations, and usually being encamped in some zareba of limited amenities'*.[7]

The aim of the Girls' Training Corps, as reported in the *Chard and Ilminster News* in 1942, was to give girls *"the preliminary training essential for any form of National Service, which, as they reach the proper age, they will be required to undertake. Their desire to serve their*

Fig 7. W.J.A.C. Emergency Feeding Post rehearsal. Many of the girls would become members of the Women's Voluntary Service which provided emergency feeding stations.

Fig 8. 254 Company Girl's Training Corps musicians on parade and providing a fanfare for the arrival of a V.I.P.

Fig 9. W.J.A.C. cadets learning to fight fires with the aid of the local fire brigade, 1945.

country is no less than that of their brothers whose imagination has been fired by enrolment in the A.T.C. and the A.C.F."[8] There was a secondary purpose and that was to *"offer scope for all talents and enable girls to find out in advance for which form of National Service they are best fitted"*. Suffice it to say that the Girls' National Training Corps, with its three

Fig 10. Derek McCulloch known nationally as 'Uncle Mac' (Children's BBC radio presenter and Home Guard officer) presents ability badges to W.J.A.C. cadets, 1943.

different Service affiliations, gave those girls who wished to involve themselves in a nationally-organised and semi-military way, the opportunity to feel that they were 'doing their bit' for King and country at a time of national emergency.

Initially it was envisaged that the enrolment age would be 16 years, this being the age at which youngsters were to register under the Governmental National Service scheme but this was lowered to 14, in line with the age of enrolment for male cadets. The age of 'retirement' as a cadet was 20.

When the war ended in 1945 plans were put forward to close down the Corps but the membership had other plans. Programmes were up-dated and modified to fit post-war life.

If the invaluable service given to the county during the Second World War by the C.C.F., the S.C.C., the A.C.F., and the A.T.C., is little known then this is doubly so when the efforts and effect of the National Association of Training Corps for Girls, with its three organisations, is considered. The formation of the girls' organisations not only benefited the cadets. The Government was pleased at the response to recruitment as it helped to cater for youngsters and provide for them a suitable outlet for their energies in a way that helped the country. The formation of the N.A.T.C.G., must also have given the organisers and their officers an opportunity to 'do their bit'. Not surprisingly, most of the Corps' officers came from the professional and middle classes; a large number were teachers, doctors and titled ladies, and nearly all the secretaries were, because it was a Board of Education run organisation, members of the Local Education Authorities.

In 1955 H.R.H. Princess Alexandra became the Corps Patron. In 1963 the Girls' Nautical Training Corps joined the Sea Cadet Corps, and the other two amalgamated in 1964 to form the Girls' Venture Corps, the words 'Air Cadets' being added in 1987. The latter still exists to this day.

CHAPTER 4

TRAINING FOR GIRLS

ILLUSTRATIONS

CHAPTER FIVE

ON PARADE AND IN THE PUBLIC EYE

With well over half a million boys and girls in military uniform, it was no surprise that cadets were noticed, and they were often called upon to perform public duties. The regular and reserve forces were engaged in pressing matters to do with the war, which left a vacuum. Who, for example was to take part in the Remembrance Day parades up and down the country on the 11th November? The Home Guard might be engaged and not available, so who was left? And who would accommodate any local function, or functionary who required a parade? The cadets. The cadet units which had a band were in great demand, as indeed they still are today.

Fig 1. 1st Isle Drums A.C.F. band from Wisbech and Whittlesey units in Wisbech Park, 1945.

Fig 2. Gravesend A.T.C. Squadron with the local W.J.A.C. band members, c.1945.

Fig 3. Drum majors from the A.T.C. and W.J.A.C. getting last minute instructions.

The bands on parade did not always belong to a single cadet organisation and given the paucity of adult musicians it made sense to share bandmasters and instructors.

Fig 4. Girls also get help from the sea cadets. Cadet Petty Officer Yarrow shows the W.J.A.C. girls from Streatham how to play the bugle.

The size of many of the cadet units – those in the larger towns could be well over 100 in number – meant that their parades and inspections were held in spacious public places, and as the regular forces and reserves had little time to parade the 'top brass' took advantage of these opportunities to inspect such large bodies of uniformed individuals.

It was not uncommon for the highest-ranking officers to inspect the Junior Training Corps contingents at the public schools as some of the inspectors may well have been 'old boys' of the school; Mr W. W. Wakefield M.P. the Director of the A.T.C., for example, was an ex-pupil of Sedbergh School. Visits and inspections were always 'grand' occasions made doubly so with ex-pupils keeping in touch with the school they had recently left and imparting their news; most of the schools kept a record of their old-boys' wartime achievements. Schools were very proud of any ex-pupil who was awarded a high military honour and if the recipient was a holder of the Victoria Cross, his name would be for ever etched at the top of the school's memorial list. The J.T.C. school archives are mostly well kept. The open units, alas, did not have the facilities for maintaining records; besides which their membership was transitory. Suffice it to say that the large number of ex-S.C.C., A.C.F. and A.T.C. cadets who distinguished themselves during the prolonged conflict of the Second World War is, alas, unrecorded.

The Royal Navy never forgets Nelson's great victory at Trafalgar. In 1945, when the war in Europe was finally over, the Sea Cadet Corps, under the auspices of the Navy League, celebrated the 140th anniversary of Nelson's triumph, in the famous eponymous square in London. The 1945 Trafalgar Day programme ended with a Jubilee and Victory concert at

Fig 5. Earl Harewood inspects J.T.C. Guard of Honour at Sedbergh School, 1944. There were 380 cadets on parade; practically every boy in the school was a member of the Junior Training Corps. Training displays included breaching a minefield and weapon training.

the Coliseum, and a luncheon for the Navy League representatives and V.I.P. guests at the Savoy Hotel. Proceeds from all the celebratory functions were used to swell the coffers of the Sea Cadet Corps.[1]

Public parades were often used as a means of raising funds for the war effort. Each year the Government launched a drive specifically to help collect money for one of the armed services. Town councils would publish a monetary target that they aimed to reach within a week. In 1941 there was *War Weapons Week*; in 1942 it was *Warship Week*, followed in 1943 by *Wings for Victory*; and in 1944 there was *Salute the Soldier Week*. As an incentive,

Fig 6. *Sea Cadets on parade for the 140th anniversary of Trafalgar Day, 1945.*

Fig 7. *Nelson's Prayer was read by Leading Cadet Arthur Mann of the St. Clement Dane's Unit. Others in the picture are Vice Admiral C. C. Morgan, Admiral Commanding Reserves; Admiral Sir Lionel Halsey, Chairman of the Navy League and Mr. H.T. Bishop, General Secretary of the Navy League.*

prizes were given for the town that raised the most funds within each district, and in Somerset there was the county's 'Small Savings' flag for the smaller, more rural towns and villages.[2]

It is impossible to say how much each cadet unit contributed to the fund raising. It is known, however, that in 1943 the City of Salford Air Training Corps Wing raised £20,286. In the same year the more affluent area encompassing the North East Surrey Air Training Corps Wing *'centred on wealthy Wimbledon'* collected over £50,000 *'of which'*, it was reported in the *Air Training Corps Gazette*, *'over £1,000 was contributed by the cadets personally'*. Cadets were also used as collectors for a number of other good causes. It was reported in the *Sea Cadet* magazine that in 1940 the sea cadets of York collected cash to

Fig 8. Mrs Alexander, wife of the First Lord of the Admiralty, making a donation, 1944.

buy *'comforts for the Navy'*. The cadets' contribution was sometimes more practical in nature. They provided refreshments or acted as attendants of various sorts at different functions – as they do today – or organised dances as they did in the towns of Ilminster and Chard in Somerset. The latter helped to raise £124,143 which, reported the local paper, was used to equip and maintain a Somerset Light Infantry company for a year.[3]

In April 1944, in aid of *Salute the Soldier Week*, the A.C.F. Company in Hitchin, Hertfordshire joined a parade which included H.M. Forces and the United States Air Force. Following the parade, the A.C.F. cadets put on a display in the Town Square, each platoon featured a different aspect of training. There was rifle drill, P.T., a section attack, drill with a Sten sub-machine gun and even an assault course competition.

It was recorded in the *Army Cadet Journal* that the Director of the Home Guard and the A.C.F., Lord Bridgeman, asked the people of Hitchin to salute *'the soldiers, the part-time soldiers*

Fig 9. Sten Gun display by cadets of Hitchin A.C.F. Company in the Town Square for Salute the Soldier Week, 1944.

Fig 10. Assault course competition for A.C.F. cadets during a display to raise money for Salute the Soldier Week fund at Hitchin, Hertfordshire in 1944.

of the Home Guard, and the soldiers of the future (the A.C.F.)' by giving generously. The incredibly large target of £250,000 was surpassed within a week.[4] In London fund-raising efforts were often more elaborate. In 1943 one of the Government's Mass Observation operatives described the efforts to raise money for the *Wings for Victory* campaign in Trafalgar Square. A Lancaster bomber was grandly placed on a high platform above the crowds, and, wrote the operative: *"Such crowds of people. Men selling flags and baubles. Music playing and soldiers in a jeep going round and round the square. There were firemen selling odd stamps to put on the bomber, and in the fountain some air cadets were shouting and enjoying themselves. They were paddling around in a rubber dinghy such as wrecked airmen use and people threw pennies to them".*[5]

The dignitaries and VIPs who visited and reviewed the cadets included men of senior military rank and members of foreign aristocracies. Exiled Royals accepted the opportunity to be seen fulfilling their public role. King Haakon of Norway appears to have been a popular choice to inspect cadets, so too was the young King Peter of Yugoslavia.

Fig 11. King Haakon of Norway visits 285 Sqn. (Purley & Coulsdon) in Surrey, 1942.

Parades and displays invariably included the obligatory inspection and occasionally a more

Fig 12. H.M. King Haakon also visited the Sea Cadets. He is seen here inspecting No. 23 Barrow S.C.C. unit, c.1942.

unusual and enterprising performance would be seen. King Haakon, on his visit in 1942 to No. 285 Squadron A.T.C., was treated to a pre-modern day 'Red Arrows' type display, with cadets executing their formation 'flying' on bicycles.[6]

A public parade is always an occasion to look one's best, 'strut one's stuff' and feel proud. Nowhere is this better felt than when marching behind a band, and for some, this is partic-ularly true if it is a pipe band.

Fig 13. 285 (Purley & Coulsdon) Squadron A.T.C. 'display team' attacks the enemy in formation during a visit by the King Haakon of Norway, 1942.

45

Cadets and the War, 1939–1945

Fig 14. Team leader of the attacking formation team of No. 285 Squadron A.T.C., 1942.

Fig 15. Kensington S.C.C. unit keeping up tradition, seen here raising the flag, 1943.

The number of visits by high-ranking officers underlined the importance and regard that the Armed Forces had for the Cadet Movement, and when the visitor was a well-known senior officer, that cadet organisation felt that it was definitely appreciated and contributing to the war effort in a meaningful way. The War Office, the Admiralty and the Air Ministry were, of course, looking to their future but they were also mindful that the presence of bands and patriotic displays served as morale boosters for everyone, as well as completing the programme for a visiting dignitary.

There was no system in place to log the total number of visits by dignitaries to the various cadet organisations. Pictorial evidence suggests, however, that there was quite a number and that they were undertaken at regular intervals. The units located in the cities or near

Fig 16. General Montgomery, Britain's best known soldier visits the A.C.F. in 1944.

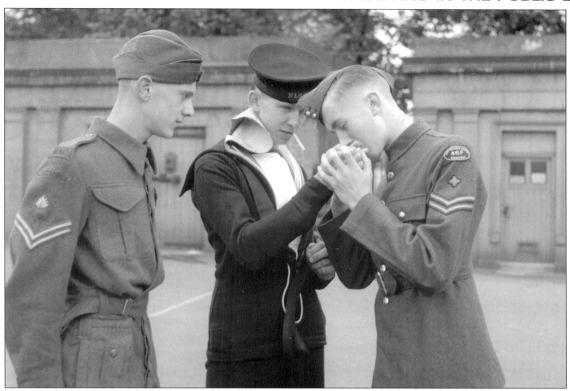

Fig 17. S.C.C., A.C.F. and A.T.C. cadets relaxing prior to an inter-services parade 1942. There were 6,000 cadets on parade in London on that day.

Fig 18. Chief of Naval Information, Rear-Admiral R.H. Dickson D.S.O. inspects the Sea Cadet unit at Horley, Surrey in 1945. It is interesting to note that the cadets are parading with fixed bayonets, a privilege usually given only to units which had been granted the 'freedom of the town or city'.

Fig 19. 'Never in the field of human conflict have so few been inspected by so many'.

various Armed Services headquarters probably received more than their fair share of visitations. A cartoon in the *Air Cadet Gazette* of 1943 by 'Quix' parodies Churchill's famous speech and in so doing suggests that perhaps there were too many inspections, with too many inspectors.

CHAPTER 5

ON PARADE AND IN THE PUBLIC EYE

ILLUSTRATIONS

Fig 1. 1st Isle Drums A.C.F. band from Wisbech and Whittlesey units in
Wisbech Park, 1945.
Company Commander's Log Book 1942–1949, (unpublished)
Whittlesey Army Cadets Association.

Fig 2. Gravesend A.T.C. Sqn with the local W.J.A.C. band members, c. 1945.
Girls' Venture Corps Air Cadets' archives.

Fig 3. Drum majors from the A.T.C. and W.J.A.C. getting last minute instruction.
Girls Venture Corps Air Cadets' archives.

Fig 4. W.J.A.C. girls also get help from the Sea Cadets. Cadet Petty Officer Yarrow
shows the W.J.A.C. girls from Streatham how to play the bugle.
Girls Venture Corps Air Cadets' archives.

Fig 5. Earl Harewood inspects Junior Training Corps cadets at Sedbergh
School, 1944.
Photograph reproduced courtesy of the *Westmorland Gazette*, the
premier newspaper of The Lakes.

Fig 6. Sea Cadets on parade for the 140th anniversary of Trafalgar Day, 1945.
The Sea Cadet Journal, 1945.

Fig 7. Fig 7. Nelson's Prayer was read by Leading Cadet Arthur Mann of the St.
Clement Dane's Unit. Others in the picture are Vice Admiral C. C. Morgan,
Admiral Commanding Reserves; Admiral Sir Lionel Halsey, Chairman of the
Navy League and Mr. H.T. Bishop, General Secretary of the Navy League.
The Sea Cadet Journal, 1945.

Fig 8. Mrs Alexander, wife of the First Lord of the Admiralty, making a donation,
1944.
Imperial War Museum, Ref. A22594.

Fig 9. Sten Gun display by cadets of A.C.F. Hitchin company in the Town
Square for *Salute the Soldier Week*, 1944.
Hertfordshire Pictorial, 1944.

Fig 10. Assault course competition for A.C.F. cadets during a display to raise
money for *Salute the Soldier Week*, at Hitchin, Hertfordshire in 1944.
Hertfordshire Pictorial, 1944.

Fig 11. H. M. King Haakon of Norway visits 285 Squadron (Purley & Coulsdon) 1942.
Air Cadets Corps Gazette, 1942.

Cadets and the War, 1939–1945

Fig 12. H. M. King Haakon also visited the Sea Cadets. He is seen here inspecting the Barrow S.C.C. unit, c. 1942.
The Sea Cadet Journal, 1942

Fig 13. 285 (Purley & Coulsdon) Squadron 'display team' attacks the enemy in formation, during a visit by the King of Norway, 1942.
Air Cadets Corps Gazette, 1942.

Fig 14. Team leader of the No. 285 Squadron's attacking formation team, 1942.
Air Cadets Corps Gazette, 1942.

Fig 15. Kensington SCC unit keeping up tradition, seen here raising the flag, 1943.
The Sea Cadet Journal, 1943.

Fig 16. General Montgomery, Britain's best known soldier visits the A.C.F. in 1944.
Army Cadet Journal, 1945.

Fig 17. S.C.C., A.C.F. and A.T.C. cadets relaxing prior to an inter-services Parade, 1942.
Imperial War Museum, Ref. H21153.

Fig 18. Chief of Naval Information, Rear Admiral R.H. Dickson D.S.O. inspects *the* Sea Cadet unit at Horley, Surrey in 1945. It is interesting to note that the cadets are parading with fixed bayonets, a privilege usually given only to units which had been granted the 'freedom of the town' or city'.
Imperial War Museum, Ref. A28983.

Fig 19. 'Never in the field of human conflict have so few been inspected by so many'.
Air Training Corps Gazette, 1943.

CHAPTER SIX

BASIC MILITARY TRAINING

The aim was always to make training as realistic and, especially in wartime, as relevant as possible. Learning to shoot and handle weapons was regarded as a necessary skill. Shooting the ·22 bolt-action No. 8 rifle was part of the Army Cadet syllabus and all pre-service cadets leant how to handle the military issue Lee Enfield ·303 rifle.

Fig 1. Army Cadet NCO teaching a recruit to shoot with the ·22 calibre No. 8 rifle.

Fig 2. Army Cadet NCO instructing cadets on how to strip a Sten Sub-machine Gun.

Following Dunkirk, where much of the army's weaponry was left on the French beaches, the A.C.F. was ordered to give its weapons to the expanding citizens' army, the Home Guard.[1] The Lee Enfield rifles and the Bren Machine Guns were handed over immediately on request. Initially the Home Guard had very few weapons; indeed some, like the Rickmansworth Home Guard, toted pikes in 1940. However, there was great excitement when the unit with its cadets went to see a demonstration of a new weapon in a field nearby at Northwood. It was a drainpipe which had a spike secured inside at one end and two struts to hold it steady in the ground. It was, in effect, a very rudimentary mortar gun that

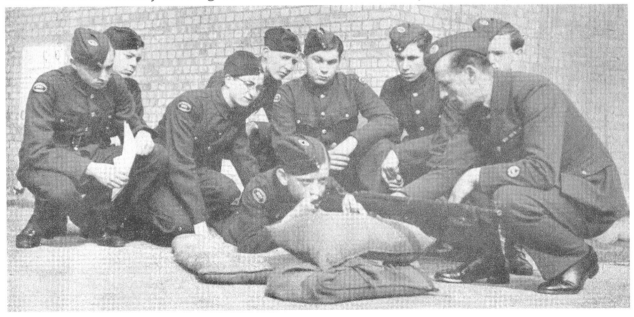

Fig 3. Air Cadets receiving training with a ·303 calibre rifle.

Cadets and the War, 1939–1945

Fig 4. *The 4th Cadet Bn. The Queen's Regt. in mock attack at a Combined Cadet Display at Coulsdon, Surrey, 1944.*

was supposed to fire home-made 'shells' in the form of milk bottles filled with stones! The Home Guard in turn gave some of their weapons to the army until the deficit was made up. The replacement weapons for the cadets were Martini-Henry carbines, some of which had an interesting history. The 100 carbines issued to the Junior Training Corps at Birkenhead School had last been used at Rorke's Drift in 1879.[2] This single-shot rifle could fire off twelve rounds a minute, that is if they did not jam. Later the Lee Enfield rifle became more readily available and in 1942 the cheaply manufactured Sten sub-machine gun superseded the Bren Light Machine Gun issue for cadet units.

Many of the cadets, particularly the army cadets, become members of the Home Guard. Thus the skills and weapons they had learnt about with the Home Guard were used to train cadets. The A.T.C. and the girls' units also took advantage of the Home Guard instruction. Many of the instructors were ex-First World War military instructors, and they provided weapon training for the cadets.

The army-badged Royal Artillery cadet detachments and the Sea Cadets Corps that had field guns continued to practise gunnery skills. With the Armed Forces taking greater control of the training programmes, more cadets were receiving familiarisation with more advanced

Fig 5. *W.J.A.C. cadets given a practical lesson on aircraft armaments, c.1944.*

THE NAVY LEAGUE

Certificate

of

PROFICIENCY FOR CADET SEAMAN-GUNNER

This is to Certify

THAT CADET _D. H. White._

OF THE _Hendon._ SEA CADET CORPS HAS UNDERTAKEN AN ELEMENTARY COURSE OF GUNNERY INSTRUCTION AS DETAILED BELOW, AND HAS PASSED AN EXAMINATION OF PROFICIENCY. _Superior performance._

12 pdr. 12 cwt.	Component Parts, Care and Maintenance. Gun Drill for A.A. Barrage and Surface Targets. Ammunition.
4 in. B.L.	Component Parts, Care and Maintenance. Use of Sights. Elementary Fire Control, including use of the Dumaresq and Vickers Range Clock. Ammunition. ·303 Lewis M/Gun. 0·5 Colt Browning M/Gun. Oerlikon C/Gun. ·38 Revolver. 9 M/M Lanchester.

Lieutenant-Commander, R.N.V.R.
S.C.G.O.

Fig 6. Certificate [1943] showing range of Gunnery training undertaken by S.C.C. Cadet D. White of Hendon.

Cadets and the War, 1939–1945

Fig 7. *Northampton Sea Cadets at Field Gun practice, c.1943.*

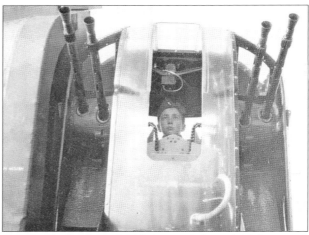

Fig 8. *Cadet from 2112 (Luton) Sqn. A.T.C. trying out the rear turret of a Wellington bomber.*

weapons. Not only did this promote interest, it also speeded up the training once those cadets had moved on to serve with the Royal Navy, Army or Royal Air Force. Gunnery training became a recognised part of the Sea Cadet Corps training programme, in particular.

The Sea Cadets, particularly those with inland headquarters, tried to re-create the reality of service life. They did this by modelling their headquarters – known as Training Ships – to simulate on-board conditions. An excellent example was the *T.S. Undaunted* at Bromley.

The training for a Sea Cadet at his twice-weekly parades consisted of five basic components: signals and flags, discipline, fitness, citizenship and seamanship. A cadet's educational standard, although not part of the S.C.C., training, was noted. It was an important consideration for those who had ambitions to command, and wanted to be officers in the

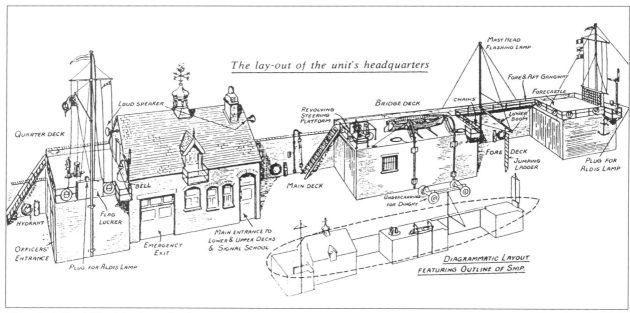

Fig 9. *The* T.S. Undaunted *comprised upper and lower decks. An adjoining hall under the quarterdeck was the ship's office, library, bosun's and clothing stores, plus armoury. At the upper deck was the signal school. On the quarterdeck stood the ship's wheel, steering platform, binnacle, ship's bell, lofty mast, flag locker with semaphore. On the starboard side was fitted a 15' boat that could be lowered. Electrical cables connected both signals stations, so communication by Aldis lamp was possible. Orthodox ship's rails and lifeboats were also fitted, and the bridge deck had a revolving steering platform.*

future. The aim was, of course, to combine the spirit of team-work as experienced in the Royal Navy with the learning of basic nautical skills, whilst at the same time training cadets in the ways of good citizenship.

A good example of the use of imagination and ingenuity in the provision of training aids was seen at Unit 97, Croydon (West) [Figs 10 and 11]. The unit acquired a teak-built 18' derelict, Merchant Navy lifeboat. A

Fig 10. Manning the Falls at the Croydon (West) S.C.C. unit.

pair of davits was erected to hoist the boat, and a specially constructed wooden cradle mounted on castors enabled the boat, when lowered, to be run away. Apart from the brick piers, suitably reinforced with rods and the fitting of guide collars and sole plates, the whole rigging was carried out by cadets under the supervision of officers and instructors.

Fig 11. Sail Drill ashore at the Croydon (West) unit, 1943.

The cadets learnt the technical names of the parts and how to rig the sails, to hoist and lower the boat. The customary Service orders were adhered to. The cadets were also able to do 'Dry-land' boat-pulling practice.[3]

Given the paucity of equipment, it was necessary to make or 'scrounge' pieces of kit that could be adapted to make other essential bits of equipment for training such as an Aldis lamp or a radio receiver.

Those Army Cadet units who had a Commanding Officer, adult instructor or senior Cadet NCO serving with a Home Guard detachment, had the benefit of training with weapons, such as the Lewis Machine Gun, which were not normally available to the cadets.

Fig 12. J.T.C. cadet at Rugby School crossing the river.

Fig 13. Army Cadets receiving instruction on the Lewis Machine Gun.

The Army Cadets made use of the countryside and tried to simulate some of the more arduous conditions a soldier might face in training, such as river crossing – without a boat – and doing manoeuvres whist wearing a claustrophobic gas mask.[4]

The emphasis was on 'hands-on', practical training with the aim of promoting, as stated in the training manual *"... that spirit of aggressive determination and self-reliance which characterises the ideal trained private soldier, and eventually the ideal leader"*.

It was stated boldly in the Sea Cadet Corps Handbook that the Corps was *"first and foremost a pre-entry training organisation"*.[5] Later, when the tide of war was turning in favour of the Allies and the need for pre-entry training lessened, the aims of the Cadet Movement were to become more embracing and included preparation for citizenship in a broader sense.

Each of the cadet organisations concentrated on their primary subjects; for the S.C.C. it was: seamanship, knots, soundings,

Fig 14. Twins from Cheshire Army Cadet Force undergoing map reading instruction given by Cadet Sergeant Bradford, the senior cadet NCO, 1942.

compass, boats and gear, rigging and 'Rules of the Road' (steering, rights of way); for the A.C.F. it was fieldcraft, map reading, skill-at-arms; the A.T.C. programme included principles of flight, navigation, propulsion and engines. Of course, each organisation did more than was on the syllabus. The width and depth of training were dependent on the skill and ingenuity of the officers and instructors and the availability of resources.

The year 1942 was crucial in the development of training for cadets. It was in 1942 that the Admiralty took complete control of Sea Cadet training. At the same time the War Office re-organised the Army Cadet syllabus and introduced formal technical training. And by 1942 the Air Training Corps had become established and training pamphlets for cadets were produced. It was also the year in which the three distinct cadet organisations for girls were started, and it was the time of the greatest growth in units and numbers, with the total membership of cadet organisations passing the half million mark.

The older school teachers, (the younger ones being in the Armed Forces) made a considerable contribution to the specific training of the cadets, particularly those requiring mathematical and scientific skills. It was no accident that many of the officers in the Air Training Corps were school masters.

School premises became the head-quarters of many of the newly-formed cadet units and so full use was made of their facilities; the playground became the parade ground, *ad hoc* assault courses were erected on playing

Fig 15. Rugby School cadets training for a gas attack in 1940.

Fig 16. Air cadets receiving instruction in navigation.

Fig 17. Cadets undergoing fieldcraft training, 1942.

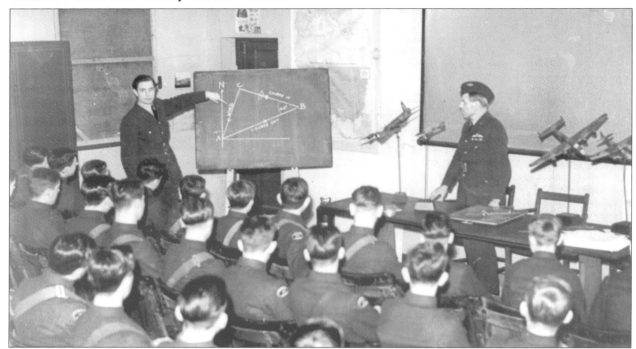

Fig 18. A.T.C. making use of school facilities for lessons in Principles of Flight.

fields and classrooms were opened in the evenings and at weekends for instruction in military subjects. In some cases, swimming pools were used for survival or amphibious assault training.

With the enormous growth in cadet establishments and more and more men being called-up the pressure was on to find officers and instructors. The Home Guard helped but could not carry out their duties and at the same time satisfactorily accommodate the burgeoning cadet units many of which were over a hundred strong. Schoolmasters could, and they were used, but they needed military training, and old soldiers, ex-sailors and airmen needed revision courses. With the Armed Forces now dictating the training of cadets, it was up to the

Fig 19. Lt. Harold Wyllie, OBE, R.N.V.R., 64-year-old son of the famous artist the late William Wyllie, RA, giving seamanship instruction to a class of Sea Cadet officers at Portsmouth, 1944.

Front Row (left to right)—Lieutenants A. D. Howman-Meek (Weymouth). T. F. Kirkpatrick (Belfast). W. H. Nash-Brown (Elham Valley). J. M. Wilcox (Blackburn). Lt.-Commander C. L. A. Woollard (District Officer. West Kent). Lieutenants A. McT. Short (Cardiff). A. J. Guthrie (Glasgow). D. Potter (Seven Sisters. Wales). J. A. Goodbrand (Edinburgh).
Second Row (standing)—Sub-Lieutenants R. Thorn (Tyne). A. H. Horrocks (Kettering). H. C. Arrowsmith (Stoke-on-Trent). T. G. King (Belfast). T. Ellam (Orpington). B. G. Shrine (Kettering). N. Hearsey (Buxton). J. S. C. Masson (Carshalton). F. Aldis (Woolwich).
Back Row—Sub-Lieutenants G. Warn (Halifax). J. Mair (Belfast). J. Cotton (Hornsey, London). C. Stephenson (Hebburn-on-Tyne).

Fig 20. Participants in the first Sea Cadet Officers' course. In 1942/43 courses for officers and Chief Petty Officers were held on H.M.S. Foudroyant, *the S.C.C. headquarters afloat, under the Commanding Officer, Lieutenant Commander P. O'Brian R.N.*

War Office, Admiralty and Air Ministry to provide training for officers. In 1942 the Royal Naval College, Greenwich, staged the first Sea Cadet officers' training course. It lasted a fortnight and included lectures on: traditions and customs of the Royal Navy, leadership, King's Regulations and Admiralty Instructions, seamanship, navigation, and how to behave in the Ward Room.[6] The latter was euphemistically known as the 'knife and fork' course.

Increasingly, with officers leaving for active service and the calling up of younger adults into the military, the onus of instruction fell on the shoulders of inexperienced officers. And some officers, being 70 years old, were well beyond retirement age. The idea of a retirement age was mooted by the Sea Cadets but it was thought expedient to have an enthusiastic old sea-dog at the helm rather than close a unit for want of leadership.

The loss of trained adult personnel, particularly in the first two years of war, was considerable. In the 1st Cadet Bn. The Royal Fusiliers (City of London Regt.) 20 of the 28 officers had gained commissions in the Army. The War Office had to do something and in 1941 week-long courses were held at Pirbright, Malvern and Oxford for Army Cadet officers. The syllabus included the expected military skills training plus lectures on *'Tanks and Support Arms, Gas, Man Management, Hygiene and Message and Report Writing'.*[7] The initial appointment of Mr J.F. Wolfenden, Headmaster of Uppingham School, as Director of Pre-Entry Training for the A.T.C. was an inspired decision. He understood and spoke the language of county education authorities and was able to solicit help from the Board of Education.[8] As a result, teachers in colleges, schools and evening institutes gave extra classes mainly in English, mathematics and meteorology. It was not surprising therefore that fifty per cent of A.T.C. officers were teachers.

Week-long officer training courses for A.T.C. personnel were begun in 1942, with Loughborough College running a Summer School to train officers in elementary and advanced aeronautics.

Fig. 21. Air Chief Marshal Sir Robert Brooke-Popham with officers of the first commanding officers' course at St. Andrew's, Edinburgh in 1942. Later in 1942 R.A.F. Cosford was to become the regular venue for the training of officers.

Many of the school teachers were dual-hatted as they already had commissions with the Home Guard. However, public recognition of the importance of training the youth for future service in the Armed Forces came in 1942 when the status of officers changed. Officers in the A.C.F. were granted Commissions in the Territorial Army Reserve and A.T.C. Officers in the Royal Air Force Reserve [Training Branch], although the Sea Cadet Corps preferred to make theirs an Admiralty appointment.

Fig 22. Schoolmasters at Sedbergh School being introduced to Lord Harewood at the J.T.C.'s annual inspection in 1944. Schoolmasters were, naturally, the main source of officer personnel for the J.T.C., and increasingly teachers played a role in the training of all cadets, their expertise being needed particularly for technical and academic subjects.

By 1944 questions were being asked in Parliament regarding the future of the Cadet Movement. This was partly prompted by the report in the *Daily Mail* in 1944, stating that the Government was intending to introduce a scheme for compulsory enrolment of boys into pre-Service organisations. This was pure speculation. The cadet organisations *'needed no artificial aids to prosperity'* – recruitment was not a problem. The aims of the organisations were broad and encompassed the Government's concern regarding training for citizenship. If the cadet organisations were concerned about future recognition, financial support and military assistance after the war, they had no need to worry. With the continuation of National Service for all males aged 18 and added interest from the education authorities in the form of the 1944 Education Act, there was a concern for the future of the county in peace time. Included in this concern was the development of what had come to be called *"The Service of Youth"*.[9] In May, 1943 a conference for Youth Leaders was held at Shrewsbury at which the Cadet Services were represented by Major General Bridgeman, officer commanding the Home Guard and Army Cadets. Concern was expressed at the attitude of some cadet officers who only saw cadet training in terms of its military benefits. General Bridgeman emphasised that the Cadet Services *'were not imitations of the other Services but preparation for them'*. It was clear that Social Education was more important in war time *'because of the difference in home life with the father in the Forces and the mother in war work'*. The boys were not necessarily going to become soldiers but citizens, therefore everyone agreed that the *'needs of future citizenship would not be served by military training alone'*.[10]

In the interim, basic military training was still required but there was an awareness of the future and the needs of the next generation. This was echoed by the Deputy Prime Minister, the Rt. Hon. C R Attlee M.P., in a Foreword to *The Cadet Journal* in 1944, in which he said:

> *It is, therefore, a pleasure to me to send a message to the cadets of today in the midst of the greatest war in history. I am certain that you are learning self discipline and leadership which will help you to serve the country in war and peace.*

CHAPTER 6

BASIC MILITARY TRAINING

ILLUSTRATIONS

Fig 1.   Army Cadet NCO teaching a recruit to shoot with the ·22 calibre No. 8 rifle.
Still photo from the *Three Cadets*, 1944 film, Greenpark Productions.

Fig 2.   Army Cadet NCO instructing cadets how to strip a Sten Sub-machine Gun.
Still photo from the *Three Cadets*, 1944 film, Greenpark Productions.

Fig 3.   Air Cadets receiving training with a ·303 calibre rifle.
Air Ministry, *The Story of the Air Training Corps* (Air League of the British Empire, 1946).

Fig 4.   4th Cadet Bn. The Queen's Regt. in mock attack at a Combined Cadet.
Display at Coulsdon, Surrey, 1944.
Army Cadet Journal, 1944.

Fig 5.   Cadets of the W.J.A.C. inspecting aircraft machine guns when on a visit to an arms factory, c. 1944.
Girls Venture Corps Air Cadets' archives.

Fig 6.   Certificate showing range of Gunnery training undertaken by S.C.C.
D.H. White.

Fig 7.   Northampton Sea Cadets at gunnery practice.
C.P.O. S. Tilley, Northampton Sea Cadets, c.1943.

Fig 8.   Air Cadet from 2112 (Luton) Sqn. in the rear turret of a Wellington Bomber.
Air Training Corps Gazette, 1945.

Fig 9.   Line drawing of *T. S. Undaunted*.
The Sea Cadet Journal, 1944.

Fig 10 .   Manning the Falls at the Croydon (West) unit.
The Sea Cadet Journal, 1943.

Fig 11.   Sail Drill ashore at the Croydon (West) unit, 1943.
ibid.

Fig 12 .   J.T.C. cadet at Rugby School crossing the river.
Harris, Lt-Col., Rugby School Corps 1860-1960 (Brown, Knight & Truscott, 1960).

Fig 13.   Army Cadets receiving instruction on the Lewis Machine Gun.
Imperial War Museum, Ref. H9757.

Fig 14.	Twins from Cheshire A.C.F. undergoing map reading instruction in 1942.
Imperial War Museum, Ref. H22306.

Fig 15 .	Rugby School cadets training for a gas attack in 1940.
ibid.

Fig 16.	Air Cadets receiving instruction in navigation.
Air Training Corps Gazette, 1942.

Fig 17.	Army Cadets undergoing fieldcraft training, 1942.
Imperial War Museum, H22311.

Fig 18.	A.T.C. making use of school facilities for lesson in Principles of Flight.
Imperial War Museum, CH5033.

Fig 19.	Lt. Harold Wyllie OBE, R.N.V.R. giving seamanship instruction to a class
of Sea Cadet officers at Portsmouth, 1942.
Imperial War Museum, A25959.

Fig 20.	Participants in the first Sea Cadet Officers' course. In 1942/43 courses for
officers and Chief Petty Officers were held on H.M.S. Foudroyant, the S.C.C.
headquarters afloat, under the Commanding Officer, Lieutenant Commander
P. O'Brian R.N.
The Sea Cadet Journal, 1944.

Fig 21.	Air Chief Marshal Sir Robert Brooke-Popham with officers of the first
commanding officers'course at St. Andrew's, Edinburgh in 1942. Later in
1942 R.A.F. Cosford was to become the regular venue for the training of officers.
Air Training Corps Gazette, 1943.

Fig 22.	Schoolmasters at Sedbergh School being introduced to Lord Harewood
at the J.T.C's annual inspection, 1944.
Photograph reproduced by kind permission of *The Westmorland
Gazette*, 'the premier newspaper of The Lakes'.

Cadets and the War, 1939–1945

CHAPTER SEVEN

COURSES AND CAMPS

The quantity and quality of training at any cadet unit were dependent on the number of qualified instructors and the availability of equipment. They were also subject to the vagaries of war; the black-out and the blitz. The latter made travel dangerous and on occasions stopped cadets from parading. In order to give cadets a concentrated and up-to-date military training experience, the Armed Services arranged visits to military bases and put on residential courses.

The most historical of all the locations employed as bases for training cadets and officers of the Sea Cadet Corps were Nelson's two vintage warships moored in Portsmouth Harbour; *H.M.S. Implacable* and *H.M.S. Foudroyant*.

Using such ancient ships as training establishments may have seemed incongruous, but the fact that they had seen action at Trafalgar and other battles must have been a source of pride and inspiration to all who trained there.

H.M.S. Foudroyant was an ideal centre for semaphore training, flag hoisting and naval ceremony. Cadets also received training in wire splicing, rope handling, rigging work, sounding by lead and line and other basic maritime skills; the physical training took place on the wooden decks. Days were spent out on the whalers and lifeboat drill was a practiced requirement. Not surprisingly, the HQ afloat was a popular venue for annual 'camp'.[1]

Fig 1. Moored in Portsmouth Harbour were the old wooden ships H.M.S. Foudroyant *and* H.M.S. Implacable *together known as* 'H.M.S. Foudroyant', *established in June, 1943, as the training facility for Sea Cadets entering the Royal Navy and for Sea Cadet officers' courses.* H.M.S. Foudroyant *(formerly* H.M.S. Trincomalee) *was added to the training establishment in 1932. The two ships became the HQ afloat of the Corps.*

Fig 2. H.M.S. Implacable, *formerly the French 74-gun* Duguay Trouin, *had seen action at Trafalgar. It had been a training ship for boys at Devonport since 1855. Regrettably, it was scuttled after World War 2.*

No amount of training in the classroom compares with 'doing it for real'. Instruction ashore or on a moored boat was all very well as an introduction but the purpose of the training and the use of the skills learnt become obvious when afloat, and no doubt the sense of accomplishment was greater, no matter whether the cadet was doing rope-work, steering a boat or taking soundings.

The Sea Cadet Corps provided partially-trained apprentices for both the Royal Navy and the Merchant Fleet. In 1943 the Ministry of War started shortened courses at Wallasey, near Liverpool for Merchant seamen. Boys with no previous sea training were required to undertake a 10-week course before taking the tests. The ex-S.C.C. cadets, however, were able to pass the tests at the end of just four weeks of training. The majority of Sea Cadets obtained a 1st Class pass which entitled them to be rated as Junior Ordinary Seamen when they entered the Merchant Navy at 17 years of age.[2]

Provision was made for identifying the potential Royal Navy, Fleet Air Arm, Royal Marine officer and Royal Air Force pilot. This provision was known as the 'Y' Scheme. It had a threefold objective – (a) to pick out in advance the young men who, it was considered, would do well in the Navy, (b) to enable cadets to get into the Service of their choice, (c) to make sure that until they were old enough to be called up they would receive the best available type of pre-entry training.[3]

Fig 3. Sounding – heaving the lead.

Fig 4. Sea Cadet at the helm.

Fig 5. Lifeboat drill: vital training when the loss of life is considered. In the winter months of 1942 the strain due to U-boat attacks on the British fleet was immense, especially in the North Sea and the convoys to Russia.

Medical standards for inclusion in the 'Y' scheme were high and candidates had to demonstrate that they were capable educationally of reaching the School Certificate level of attainment. Cadet membership was mandatory and special consideration was given to those who had passed the Sea Cadet Corps Petty Officer examination or the Air Training Corps proficiency examination, or Parts I and II of the Army Cadet War Certificate 'A'. On entry to the

Fig 6. On the boom. A precarious way of going ashore.

Cadets and the War, 1939–1945

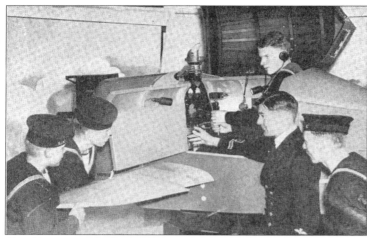

Fig 7. Future Fleet Air Arm pilots receive instruction in a Link Trainer, 1943.

'Y' scheme a Sea Cadet would formally be entered into the Navy as an unpaid reservist pending call-up, with the obligation to carry out pre-entry training with the cadets. Although a commission was not guaranteed it meant that those cadets who passed the interviews and had attained the required standards in all other respects were seen as potential officers.

The requirements of a leader were not specific to one particular Arm and the technical expertise was similar. Thus those cadets of the Sea Cadet Corps and the Air Training Corps who wanted to fly applied for entry via the 'Y' scheme, and if accepted they had a greater possibility of going into the Service of their choice.

A certain amount of homework and familiarisation training could take place at the unit's headquarters. Training under the forerunner of the A.T.C., the Air Defence Cadet Corps, was in radical need of change. The former programme was far too narrow. The basic course was broadly retained but with the formation of the A.T.C. came more stringent written tests marked by the R.A.F.'s Central Trade Board. Cadets could specialise in mathematics, Morse Code, armament, anti-gas, aircraft identification or administration. Aircrew candidates had to pass in at least three subjects, one of which must be navigation. The next best thing was to go and have a look, inspect the aircraft and get instruction from an experienced pilot. The technical ground crew candidates had a choice of specialising as wireless operators, radio mechanics, flight mechanics, instrument repairers and electricians or MT mechanics.[4]

The Air Cadet could learn about the feats of the Battle of Britain pilots, see their photographs in the *A.T.C. Gazette*, read the articles by W.E. Johns, the author of Biggles, and be stimulated by the exploits of his fictional characters, but there was no substitute for actually flying.[5]

Organised visits to R.A.F. and Fleet Air Arm stations were looked forward to by the aspirant pilots. The R.A.F. fighter pilots, following the heroics of the Battle of Britain, were christened the *'The Knights of the Air'* and the cadets wanted to meet them and to see their aeroplanes.

Motivating cadets, of whatever Service, to learn, was not too difficult. They all had a definite and realisable objective: they knew where they were heading and how to get there. The syllabuses written and produced by the different headquarters had two simple aims: first, to teach the subject-matter that the Forces required; and secondly, to re-write and present the technical texts in language easily understood by 16-year-old boys.[6]

With the aid of photographs and diagrams printed in the various cadet journals, young aspiring sailors, soldiers and airmen could gain knowledge prior to visits to active, operational units and the numbers volunteering to join the various Cadet Corps indicates that there was no shortage of young enthusiasts.

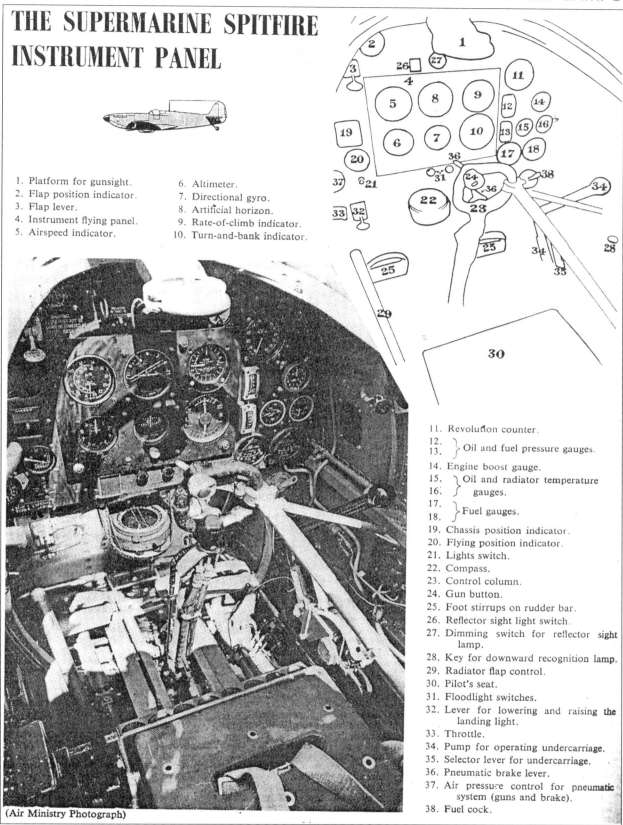

THE SUPERMARINE SPITFIRE INSTRUMENT PANEL

1. Platform for gunsight.
2. Flap position indicator.
3. Flap lever.
4. Instrument flying panel.
5. Airspeed indicator.

6. Altimeter.
7. Directional gyro.
8. Artificial horizon.
9. Rate-of-climb indicator.
10. Turn-and-bank indicator.

11. Revolution counter.
12. ⎫
13. ⎬ Oil and fuel pressure gauges.
14. Engine boost gauge.
15. ⎫ Oil and radiator temperature
16. ⎬ gauges.
17. ⎫
18. ⎬ Fuel gauges.
19. Chassis position indicator.
20. Flying position indicator.
21. Lights switch.
22. Compass.
23. Control column.
24. Gun button.
25. Foot stirrups on rudder bar.
26. Reflector sight light switch.
27. Dimming switch for reflector sight lamp.
28. Key for downward recognition lamp.
29. Radiator flap control.
30. Pilot's seat.
31. Floodlight switches.
32. Lever for lowering and raising the landing light.
33. Throttle.
34. Pump for operating undercarriage.
35. Selector lever for undercarriage.
36. Pneumatic brake lever.
37. Air pressure control for pneumatic system (guns and brake).
38. Fuel cock.

(Air Ministry Photograph)

Fig 8. Instrument and cockpit layouts, showing controls, were printed in the A.T.C. Gazette.

Every opportunity was taken to give the Cadets experience of flying in military aircraft. It was a valuable part of their training which kept them interested in aviation, and motivated them to serve in the R.A.F. or the Fleet Air Arm.

Fig 9. A.T.C. cadets getting a practical lesson from an R.A.F. Corporal technician. The Spitfire, the most agile fighter powered by a Rolls-Royce Merlin engine, was very well armed.

Aviation was still relatively new and therefore still had, to some extent, a novelty interest; besides which the R.A.F. in action was the most visible of the fighting Arms. The R.A.F. and the Fleet Air Arm had no problems with recruitment. Flying was not confined to travelling

Fig 10. Controls for the Dagling were extremely basic. The first A.T.C. Gliding School was established at Kirkbymoorside, Yorkshire, in 1942.

Fig 11. A.T.C. cadet aboard a Skeletal Dagling glider. The need for production of the Dagling was due to the R.A.F. using it specifically for training with the Air Training Corps.

in powered aircraft. Many cadets' first attempts at getting airborne were in a glider, and their maiden flight may well have been in a Skeletal Dagling glider. Maintenance of the glider was simple, so was the control and the method of launching: it relied on cadet power! This was superseded later by the use of a winch-launch for the more sophisticated Kirby Cadet Glider.

Fig 12. Not the most efficient method of launching a glider. It took sixteen cadets pulling and running flat-out to launch one cadet. This glider was not designed to fly very high.

Fig 13. *Practical demonstrations were more interesting than classroom lectures, particularly if followed by an actual flight.*

Fig 14. *A.T.C. cadets hearing first-hand what it is like to fly a sortie.*

Fig 15. Not all air experience flights were in modern aircraft, but a flight in the front seat of the cockpit of a Tiger Moth could be more exciting. During the Second World War it provided the majority of R.A.F. pilots with their elementary training and some A.T.C. and S.C.C. cadets with their first experience of flying.

Gliding experience was not confined to the Dagling 'alfresco chair lift'; it sometimes included a flight in an Airspeed Horsa Glider. The Horsa was an assault glider used in many of the airborne attacks, including the landings on Sicily and Normandy and the abortive air assault at Arnhem.

Fig 16. A.T.C. cadets kitted-out with parachutes ready for their first flight in a Wellington twin-engine medium bomber, 1944. It had a crew of six. Its top speed was 255 mph.

Cadets and the War, 1939–1945

When the cadets were visiting an airfield, harbour or training area they could spot and identify the various different craft or vehicles they had been studying back at their units. Their observation skills and ability in aircraft, ship and tank recognition could be put to the test. Each of the cadet journals published profiles of fighting machines and various modes of transportation for the cadets to learn.

Fig 17. Cadets boarding a Horsa Glider with observer parachutes and packs. The Horsa had a crew of two and could carry 20 fully-equipped soldiers. It was first deployed in 1942 and had a speed of 99 mph.

The Army Cadets also took advantage, when on visits, to look at or try out the Army's equipment and from 1944 onwards when the Allies were in the ascendancy, there were more opportunities for this. The aims of the Cadet Services, and the references in the newspapers to pre-service training differentiated the Cadet Movement from other youth organisations. The cadet units saw themselves as directly serving the war effort, although the sense of involvement varied from unit to unit and from time to time. When the cadets were away at annual camp and living in a military-style environment, their feelings of being part of the Armed Forces, and thereby contributing to the war effort, must have been heightened. Involvement in the war effort could be either civilian or military in nature. The fact that cadets operated in units and were accustomed to taking orders meant that they could easily be organised into working parties. They were utilised most effectively by the farming and forestry community, particularly during the summer months.[7]

Fig 18. Air cadets inspecting a Supermarine Walrus, a catapult-launched amphibious biplane used for reconnaissance, and search and rescue, by the Fleet Air Arm. It had a crew of three, a range of 600 miles, top speed of 135 mph, 2 x 7.7 mm machine guns and carried a 272 kg bomb.

With the unavailability of army training areas cadet units looked to farms for somewhere to train and the farmers, in turn, looked for ready labour particularly during

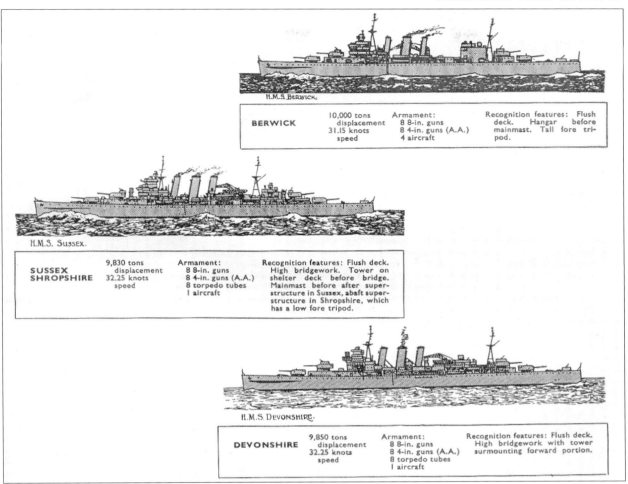

BERWICK	10,000 tons displacement 31.15 knots speed	Armament: 8 8-in. guns 8 4-in. guns (A.A.) 4 aircraft	Recognition features: Flush deck. Hangar before mainmast. Tall fore tripod.

SUSSEX SHROPSHIRE	9,830 tons displacement 32.25 knots speed	Armament: 8 8-in. guns 8 4-in. guns (A.A.) 8 torpedo tubes 1 aircraft	Recognition features: Flush deck. High bridgework. Tower on shelter deck before bridge. Mainmast before after superstructure in Sussex, abaft superstructure in Shropshire, which has a low fore tripod.

DEVONSHIRE	9,850 tons displacement 32.25 knots speed	Armament: 8 8-in. guns 8 4-in. guns (A.A.) 8 torpedo tubes 1 aircraft	Recognition features: Flush deck. High bridgework with tower surmounting forward portion.

Fig 19. Recognition of some of Britain's warships for the S.C.C.

Fig 20. Tank Identification and naming of parts for the A.C.F.

SILHOUETTES TO SCALE
SCALE 1/480 APPROX

KEY

These scale silhouettes proved very popular when we published them before.
It should be noted that the scale is only approximate.

1, Airspeed Horsa; 2, Vickers Arm-strongs Warwick; 3, Frances; 4, Super-marine Spitfire XIV; 5, Dinah; 6, North American Mitchell; 7, Hawker Tempest V; 8, Waco Hadrian; 9, Commonwealth Boomerang; 10, TB-7; 11, Mavis; 12, de Havilland Mosquito XVI; 13, Lockheed Lightning; 14, Republic Thunderbolt; 15, Glen; 16, Hawker Typhoon; 17, PE-2; 18, Jill; 19, Boeing Fortress III; 20, Judy; 21, Myrt; 22, Grumman Hellcat; 23, YAK-9; 24, Consolidated Privateer; 25, IL-2 Stormovik; 26, North Ameri-can Mustang; 27, Betty; 28, Vought Corsair; 29, Bell Airacomet.

10

Fig 21. A.T.C. squadrons would compete in Aircraft Recognition tests against each other and successfully against Royal Observer Corps units.

harvest time. The arrangement was for the unit to do cadet training on the days when the farmers did not need assistance. Thus Harvest Camps existed for the benefit of both the agricultural and the cadet communities.

There were other advantages. The War Agricultural Committee supplied a large dining tent free of charge, which served for lectures when it rained. In addition, extra rations were allowed for harvest workers. In the days of rationing, food was a great concern not least to growing youngsters. Harvest work was not just for the army cadets. The Minister of Labour called upon A.T.C. personnel who were on deferred service awaiting joining instructions from the R.A.F. to do farm work. And in 1944 the Admiral Commanding Reserves issued a memorandum urging all officers and Sea Cadets to do their duty and play their part by gathering in the crops. Even if cadets were not reaping the harvest they still obtained extra rations when away at camp.

Fig 22. A Vickers medium machine gun mounted on a Bren gun carrier. It is being inspected by cadets of the Wiltshire A.C.F. at an Army Demonstration on Salisbury Plain, 1945.

One of the greatest benefits, and perks, of attending annual camp was that there was no difference between the rations given to a cadet and those of an adult male in training. Thus the cadet would be much better fed at a training camp than at home.

At R.A.F. stations there would, more than likely, be a properly built cookhouse and kitchens. In the transitory camps on the farms and on army training grounds where facilities were basic the cadets would have to fend for themselves.

Latrines would have had to be dug; showers improvised and cooking arrangements would be *al fresco*. On the odd occasion dining arrangements were very comfortable. For example, Cheshire Cadets in 1942 were billeted in a large country mansion. The meals were prepared by the cadets, excepting

Fig 23. The menu at this R.A.F. station in 1943. Judging by the amount this cadet has on his plate, it can be seen that there was plenty to eat.

Cadets and the War, 1939–1945

Fig 24. Certificate 'T' Army Cadets inspecting a tank, 1944.

Fig 25. Young soldiers and cadets helped with the harvest.

dinners which were supplied by a local restaurant during the cadets' ten-day stay at camp.

Annual camp was very popular and the Cheshire Cadet battalion, like many others soon reached its complement and there was a long list of boys waiting to join. In fact, the majority of army cadets units were formed in the first two years of war.

There was initial, unseen competition between the harvest camp and the annual military training camp due to the opportunity for cadets to be paid for harvest work. At Shrewsbury School, the boys were given a choice between Harvest Camp – at which they were paid 6d a day (2½p!), and the military training camp. The monetary incentive could prove the greater. Cadets in rural units were expected to spend time on the farm in June, July and August and increasingly schools, particularly boarding schools spent time during the summer term on local farms doing their bit for the war effort.[8]

A cadet camp was reminiscent of army camps of old with rows and rows of tents placed in straight lines with well-defined areas for cooking, washing, a tented medical centre and a clearly defined area for parades and training. Tents were usually of the

Fig 26. London Irish Cadet Corps receiving tuition in grenade throwing.

Fig 27. Wiltshire A.C.F. cadets learning about the Mortar, 1945.

round bell-tent form with cadets sleeping on palliasses – Hessian bags filled with straw. They had two blankets each. And if they were lucky, duck boards to walk on if the ground was particularly wet. The time spent in the countryside was probably exhausting, certainly challenging, but mainly fun and for some, especially those cadets from the ports and cities, a much appreciated respite from enemy bombing.

All cadets learnt about map reading and camping and, facilities permitting, other adventurous training activities. Obstacle courses would be erected and physical training was a daily exercise. It was essential, especially for the urban-based army cadets, to get out into the countryside so that they could practise their military fieldcraft skills.

The most popular annual camps for the Sea Cadets were those spent afloat, and those located by the coast which meant access to harbours, ships and the sea. The next best were camps on a riverbank or next to a large lake or reservoir.

The more challenging the activity and the nearer it was to the actual wartime operations, as the cadets imagined it, the better. They wanted to fly; travel on an Air/Sea rescue launch; go on a voyage; fire blank and live ammunition and go on manoeuvres. However, it was not always possible for cadets to visit airfields during the first half of the war, it was not safe. The Battle of Britain needed to be won and the Allied air forces to gain air supremacy before cadets could have the experience flying in powered aircraft. When the Air Cadets did go to camp it was usually for seven days and cadets had to pay their own fare to and from the camp.[9]

Fig 28. Kit inspection for Sea Cadets, and learning how to stow their kit in a smart, sailor-like way.

For the most part, training at residential camps was the highlight of the year for the cadets, for the Armed Forces it was a means of consolidating the cadet training and it provided the opportunity to give the senior cadets advanced training. Instructions were obtained from whichever units were encamped in the vicinity. At an annual camp in

Fig 29. Camp was in a mansion in 1942 for these Cheshire Cadets and dinner arrived in metal canisters from a restaurant.

Fig 30. Girls and instructor with the W.J.A.C. Harrow unit at Denham camp in 1945.

Oxfordshire the American Army tank commanders gave instruction to army cadets from the Stock Exchange Cadet Company from London; the date is not known but it can be assumed it was prior to the D-Day Landings and the invasion of Europe by the Allies.

Annual camp was where the Sea Cadets did the majority of their seaborne activity, where the Air Cadets gained experience in flying and the Army Cadets went on manoeuvres. It was therefore a time when more specialised military training took place.

In addition to the air-borne training courses for the J.T.C. and A.C.F., as mentioned earlier, there was applied and advanced infantry training organised by the Army in 1944, when two courses on 'Town fight-

Fig 31. Reveille call at camp for Army Cadets, 1943.

ing' or Fighting in Built-Up Areas (FIBUA) as it is now known, were run. The training was carried out in a large blitzed area ('kindly provided by the Luftwaffe') somewhere in the

Fig 32. Sometimes facilities could be very basic, as for these army cadets from Cheshire in 1942.

81

Fig 33. An Army Cadet Force camp believed to be somewhere in Kent, c.1944. The regimented formation of tents divided the cadets into company lines.

Midlands. The courses consisted of short lectures, twenty-five demonstrations, practices, plays and discussions. There were mock battles, with the staff realistically dressed as

Fig 34. Army Cadets cleaning kit ready for inspection, 1944.

Fig 35. Army cadets on recce patrol watching the enemy, 1942.

Fig 36. Training facilities varied. This idyllic riverside sailing scene gives no hint of war but the writer of the original caption, not wanting to give the enemy any clues, simply wrote "Somewhere in England".

German soldiers, acting as enemy. Pyrotechnics added realism to the exercises and there were demonstrations of booby traps. Cadets climbed walls, abseiled and traversed streets across ropeways, patrolled through tunnels and had mock battles in the streets. For the enthusiastic and fit cadet it was both exciting and challenging. For the Army – in particular the infantry regiments, the airborne troops and the commandos – it meant a supply of motivated, well trained and committed recruits.[10]

Fig 37. S.S. Zara *was a screw schooner with steadying sails, built in 1900. She had the distinction of being requisitioned by the Royal Navy in both world wars. In World War I she deployed as an Auxiliary Patrol boat and was used in the search for Field Marshal Lord Kitchener after* H.M.S. Hampshire *was sunk in 1916. She was a Fleet Air Arm ship during World War II belonging to No. 764 Squadron, and was manned by Sea Cadets who provided the ship's company, duty boat's crew, mechanics, stokers and aircraft maintenance working parties; in 1943 she was manned continuously for five months by Sea Cadets.*

Occasionally, cadets shared facilities at combined camps which meant they could undertake Combined Operations. North Western Command held Combined Operations at a camp near Blackpool in 1943. The camp was in operation for a period of 12 weeks with cadet units staying for a period of a week at a time. In total, 600 cadets [300 A.C.F., 200 A.T.C. and 100 S.C.C.] attended the camp. The culminating 'Combined Op

Fig 38. A.C.F. cadets on an assault course.

Fig 39. Army Cadets from the City of London receiving instruction from an American tank commander, c.1943.

Fig 40. One of the more odd training devices called Stationary Driving Practice – of which it was said that its 'value as rehearsal for Spitfires is no doubt small…'

Fig 41. A.T.C. practising an air/sea rescue on one of the new fast rescue boats.

Fig 42. Wiltshire A.C.F. cadets undergoing Gunnery Drill practice, 1944.

Fig 43. Attacking the Gestapo headquarters at the Midlands-based training school, 1944.

was the highlight of the camp. The exercise was held in a training area that included a large lake with islands. On one of the islands the Air Cadets acted as the enemy, defending it from impending assault by 'black-faced commandos' [A.C.F. cadets]. During the battle the Sea Cadets from Fleetwood deposited a company of Army Cadets by rowing boats – acting as landing craft – on the island shore. The aim was to engage the enemy who were attempting to capture and then defend the radio station. To the accompaniment of thunder-flashes and under cover of smoke the enemy was finally defeated. The main purpose was to show the cadets the necessity of working together in a common cause and the importance of inter-service co-operation. It also gave them the chance to practise their leadership skills.

Fig 44. Army Cadets taking the opportunity to ride in a tank, following the demonstrations at an annual camp, 1944.

ANNUAL CAMP
August 5th—12th, 1944
OVERSTONE PARK, Nr. Northampton

CAMP PROGRAMME.

DAILY ROUTINE.

7 a.m.	-	Reveille	1 p.m.	- Dinner
8 a.m.	-	Breakfast	1.30 to 3 p.m.	Rest period
9.15 a.m.	-	First Parade	4.45 p.m.	- Tea
10.45 to 11.15 a.m.		Break.	7 p.m.	- Supper

Sunday, Aug. 6th   CHURCH PARADE
11 a.m.

Monday to Friday

MORNINGS. Drill, Training, Gun and Tank Demonstrations
AFTERNOONS. P.T. and Recreational Training
EVENINGS. Games, Competitions, Rifle Shooting, etc.

Bathing daily at the Swimming Pool.   Y.M.C.A. Canteens for Light Refreshments

Wednesday, Aug. 9th (Half Holiday)

Thursday, Aug. 10th

CEREMONIAL PARADE AND MARCH PAST

Inspection by Major-General G. St. G. ROBINSON, D.S.O., M.C.
Colonel The Northamptonshire Regiment

Band of The Northamptonshire Regiment

NOTICE. All Friends and Relatives are invited to attend Church Parade on
Sunday, and to see the March Past on Thursday Afternoon.
Visitors are also welcome to the Camp every day after 3 p.m.

GOD SAVE THE KING.

Fig 45. Poster for Northampton A.C.F. Annual Camp in 1944.

Fig 46. Her Majesty Queen Elizabeth inspecting 'C' Company of the 2nd Cadet Bn. The Bedfordshire and Hertfordshire Regiment at Biggleswade, 1944.

Annual camp was not just about training for a future role in the Armed Forces or about getting extra rations to eat. It was also about experiencing the camaraderie that occurs when cadets live and work closely together and about enjoying other pleasures in life such as going to the cinema. The latter was the most popular pastime of the day. If there was no cinema nearby, then cadets often devised their own theatrical productions. The fact that the

Fig 47. H. M. King George VI inspecting Air Training Corps Cadets at R.A.F. Halton in 1942.

school-leaving age was 14 meant that for most most cadets annual camp was also a respite from work and a time to have some fun.

The Northamptonshire camp programme, as outlined on the poster (Fig. 45), indicates its extent. It is similar to programmes of today, except for the inclusion of Gun and Tank Demonstrations. Visitors were welcome, which shows that owing to petrol rationing and lack of transport, the camp would need to be within the county boundary and not too far from the cadets' homes. It was not unusual for cadets to parade at their headquarters and then march several miles to camp carrying their rifle and their personal kit. Annual camp for all three services usually lasted a week.

A measure of the importance of the training of the youth and the work done by the various cadet organisations can be judged by the patronage shown by both the King and the Queen. Cadets were also visited by royalty from different nations whilst engaged in training at their annual camps.

CHAPTER 7

COURSES AND CAMPS

ILLUSTRATIONS

Fig 1.   Moored in Portsmouth Harbour were the old wooden ships *H.M.S. Foudroyant* and *H.M.S. Implacable* together known as '*H.M.S. Foudroyant*', established in June, 1943, as the training facility for Sea Cadets entering the Royal Navy and for Sea Cadet officers' courses. *H.M.S. Foudroyant* (formerly *H.M.S. Trincomalee*) was added to the training establishment in 1932. The two ships became the HQ afloat of the Corps.
Imperial War Museum, 1943. Ref. A19881.

Fig 2.   *H.M.S. Implacable*, formerly the 74-gun *Duguay Trouin*, had seen action at Trafalgar. It had been a training ship for boys at Devonport since 1855. Regrettably, it was scuttled after World War 2.
Sea Cadet Journal, 1945.

Fig 3.   Sounding – heaving the lead.
Still from the *Three Cadets* film, Greenpark Productions, 1944.

Fig 4.   Sea Cadet at the Helm.
Sea Cadet Journal, 1943.

Fig 5.   Lifeboat drill: vital training when the loss of life is considered. In the winter months of 1942 the strain due to U-boat attacks on the British fleet was immense, especially in the North Sea and the convoys to Russia.
Sea Cadet Journal, 1944.

Fig 6.   On the boom. A precarious way of going ashore, 1943.
Sea Cadet Journal, 1943.

Fig 7.   Future Fleet Air Arm pilots receive instruction in a Link Trainer.
Sea Cadet Journal, 1943.

Fig 8.   The Supermarine Spitfire Instrument Panel.
Air Training Corps Gazette, 1942.

Fig 9.   A.T.C. cadets getting a practical lesson from an R.A.F. Corporal technician. The Spitfire, the most agile fighter powered by a Rolls-Royce Merlin engine, was very well armed.
Imperial War Museum, 1942, Ref. CH5034.

Fig 10.   Controls for the Dagling were extremely basic. The first A.T.C. Gliding School was established at Kirkbymoorside, Yorkshire, in 1942.
R.A.F. Museum, Hendon. Ref. 5835-4.

Fig 11.   A.T.C. Cadet aboard a Skeletal Dagling Glider. The need for production of the Dagling was due to the R.A.F. using it specifically for training with the Air Training Corps.
R.A.F. Museum, Hendon. Ref. 5835-3.

Fig 12.   Not the most efficient way of launching a glider. It took sixteen cadets pulling and running flat-out to launch one cadet. This glider was not designed to fly very high.
R.A.F. Museum, Hendon. Ref. 5835-2.

Fig 13.   Practical demonstrations were more interesting than classroom lectures, particularly if followed by an actual flight.
Imperial War Museum, 1944, Ref. CH5031.

Fig 14.   A.T.C. cadets hearing first-hand what it is like to fly a sortie.
Air Training Corps Gazette, 1944.

Fig 15.   Not all air experience flights were in modern aircraft, but a flight in the front seat of the cockpit of a Tiger Moth could be more exciting. During the Second World War it provided the majority of R.A.F. pilots with their elementary training and some A.T.C. and S.C.C. cadets with their first experience of flying.
Imperial War Museum, 1944, Ref. CH5029.

Fig 16.   A.T.C. cadets kitted-out with parachutes ready for their first flight in a Wellington tiwn-engine medium bomber, 1944. It had a crew of six. Its top speed was 255mph.
Imperial War Museum, 1944, Ref. CH11060.

Fig 17.   Cadets boarding a Horsa Glider with observer parachutes and packs. The Horsa had a crew of two and could carry 20 fully-equipped soldiers. It was first deployed in 1942 and had a speed of 99mph.
Air Training Corps Gazette, 1945.

Fig 18.   Air cadets inspecting a Supermarine Walrus, as catapult-launched amphibious biplane used for reconnaissance, and search and rescue, by the Fleet Air Arm. It had a crew of three, a range of 600 miles, top speed of 135mph, 2 x 7.7mm machine guns and carried a 272kg. bomb.
Air Training Corps Gazette, 1943.

Fig 19.   Recognition of some of Britain's warships for the S.C.C.
Sea Cadet Journal, 1944.

Fig 20.   Tank Identification and naming of parts for the A.C.F.
Army Cadet Journal, 1944.

Fig 21.   A.T.C. squadrons would compete in Aircraft Recognition tests against each other and successfully against Royal Observer Corps units.
Air Training Corps Gazette, 1943.

Fig 22.   A Vickers medium machine gun mounted on a Bren gun carrier. It is being inspected by cadets of the Wiltshire A.C.F. at an Army Demonstration on Salisbury Plain, 1945.
Army Cadet Journal, 1945.

Cadets and the War, 1939–1945

Fig 23.   The menu at this R.A.F. station in 1943. Judging by the amount this cadet has on his plate, it can be seen that there was plenty to eat.
Air Training Corps Gazette, 1943.

Fig 24.   Certificate 'T' Army Cadets inspecting a tank, 1944.
Army Cadet Journal, 1944.

Fig 25.   Young soldiers and cadets helped with the harvest.
Picture from *Daily Mail* archives.

Fig 26.   London Irish Cadet Corps receiving tuition in grenade throwing.
Army Cadet Journal, 1942.

Fig 27.   Wiltshire A.C.F. cadets learning about the mortar, 1945.
Army Cadet Journal, 1945.

Fig 28.   Kit inspection for Sea Cadets, and learning how to stow their kit in a smart, sailor-like way.
Sea Cadet Journal, 1943.

Fig 29.   Camp was in a mansion in 1942 for these Cheshire Cadets and dinner arrived in metal canisters from a restaurant.
Imperial War Museum, Ref. H22314.

Fig 30.   Girls and instructor with the W.J.A.C. Harrow unit at Denham camp in 1945.
Girls' Venture Corps HQ archives.

Fig 31.   Reveille call at camp for Army Cadets, 1943.
Army Cadet Journal, 1943.

Fig 32.   Sometimes facilities could be very basic, as for these artmy cadets from Cheshire in 1942.
Imperial War Museum, Ref. H22321.

Fig 33.   An Army Cadet Force camp believed to be somewhere in Kent, c.1944. The regimented formation of tents divided the cadets into company lines.
Official Handbook of the A.C.F.A., 1949.

Fig 34.   Army Cadets cleaning kit ready for inspection, 1944.
Army Cadet Journal, 1944.

Fig 35.   Army Cadets on 'recce' patrol watching the enemy, 1942.
Imperial War Museum, Ref. H22313.

Fig 36.   Training facilities varied. This idyllic riverside sailing scene gives no hint of war but the writer of the original caption, not wanting to give the enemy any clues, simply wrote, "Somewhere in England".
Sea Cadet Journal, 1944.

Fig 37. *S.S. Zara* was a screw schooner with steadying sails, built in 1900. She had the distinction of being requisitioned by the Royal Navy in bot world wars. In World War I she deployed as an Auxiliary Patrol boat and was used in the search for Field Marshal Lord Kitchener after *H.M.S. Hampshire* was sunk in 1916. She was a Fleet Air Arm ship during World War II belonging to No. 764 Squadron, and was manned by Sea Cadets who provided the ship's company, duty boat's crew, mechanics, stokers and aircraft maintenance working parties; in 1943 she was manned continuously for five months by Sea Cadets. Courtesy of Capt (Retd) D.H.R White.

Fig 38. A.C.F. Cadets on an assault course.
Army Cadet Journal, 1945.

Fig 39. Army Cadets from the City of London receiving instruction from an American tank commander, c. 1943.
Milestone and Memories (Hillside Publishing Co, 1950).

Fig 40. One of the more odd training devices called Stationary Driving Practice – of which it was said that its 'value as rehearsal for Spitfires is no doubt small …'.
Air Training Corps Gazette, 1944.

Fig 41. A.T.C. practising an air/sea rescue on one of the new fast rescue boats.
Air Training Corps Gazette, 1945.

Fig 42. Wiltshire Army Cadets undergoing Gunnery Drill practice, 1944.
Army Cadet Journal, 1944.

Fig 43. Attacking the Gestapo headquarters at the Midland-based training school.
Army Cadet Journal, 1944.

Fig 44. Army Cadets taking the opportunity to ride in a tank, following the demonstrations at an annual camp.
Army Cadet Journal, 1944.

Fig 45. The poster for Northamptonshire A.C.F. camp in 1944.
Northamptonshire A.C.F.

Fig 46. Her Majesty Queen Elizabeth inspecting 'C' Company of the 2nd Cadet Bn. The Bedfordshire and Hertfordshire Regiment at Biggleswade, 1944.
Army Cadet Journal, 1944.

Fig 47. King George VI inspecting Air Training Corps Cadets at R.A.F. Halton in 1942.
Imperial War Museum, Ref. H30623.

Cadets and the War, 1939–1945

CHAPTER EIGHT

SERVICE WITH THE HOME GUARD

The Cadet Movement became an integral part of Service on the Home Front. In addition to the seasonal work at annual Harvest and Forestry Camps, there were other more regular ways in which the cadets, their instructors and their officers helped the war effort.

School premises were adapted to meet wartime needs. During the First World War, school playing fields were dug up and converted into frontline trenches, but in the Second World War the priority was for the construction of air-raid shelters to protect staff and pupils from enemy bombing. Black drapes covered all windows to ensure that no light was visible to enemy aircraft at night, and parts of playing fields were given over to the production of vegetables in order to aid food production.

Air raid drills, particularly in the city industrial areas and ports, became a regular part of school life. At Chigwell School in Essex there was a ban on the ringing of the school bell to signify the end of lessons. Instead, a boy from the Cadet Corps blew on a bugle. Presumably the bell was reserved for giving warning of an air raid. Air raids could have unforeseen effects. Should an air raid occur during an exam at Chigwell, the pupils were to descend to the basement, and were put on their honour not to discuss the exam questions!

There was always the additional danger of fire following an air raid. Students and cadets at boarding schools – where most pupils were members of the J.T.C. – were employed on

Fig 1. Sandbags filled by the boys and staff of Birkenhead School are stacked against the buildings as a means of protection against damage caused by air-raids.

Cadets and the War, 1939–1945

fire-watching duty. At Stonyhurst College the local Home Guard, 50 members of which were from the College, undertook all-night patrols on the College roof during the summer months and occasional ten-man picquet on the Fells during the winter. Subsistence Allowance was drawn for this, no doubt to the delight of the cadet members. Many cadets and their instructors in the town units worked with the Air Raid Precautions Service (A.R.P.), with many older cadets undertaking fire watching duties; this often meant being perched in an elevated position on a building in order to raise the alarm should a fire be spotted. In 1943 however, it was announced in *The Sea Cadet* journal that S.C.C. officers *'are exempt from fireguard duties at business premises except during working hours'*. In the area in which they lived they

Fig 2. A.T.C. cadets refuelling a bomber.

could be called upon to *'do duty only as a member of a street fire party'*. The exemption also applied to adult instructors and cadets in full-time employment, providing they attended the unit on three days a week. This shows that by 1943 participation in a pre-service cadet organisation was considered a significant wartime duty.

Wartime service for the cadets could involve working directly with the military. Middlesex A.C.F. cadets, for example, were employed to fill sandbags, and to move barbed-wire pickets as well as shift stores at the Greenford Depot, where they helped the medically down-graded servicemen waiting to be transferred to the Pioneer Corps.

The Home Guard could and did make use of the cadet facilities, such as the indoor 25-yard rifle ranges at some of the public and grammar schools. And on occasions cadets were deployed on exercises with the Army. In 1943 Stonyhurst College combined with the Royal Engineers to demonstrate a platoon attack which included crossing one of the lakes in the College grounds in assault craft, under cover of smoke and with fire support, the clearing of a mine field and the breaching of barbed wire defences with Bangalore Torpedoes.[1]

It was not unusual for cadets to assist with routine tasks when visiting a military base. Air Cadets could be usefully employed assisting in the refuelling of aircraft and Army Cadets would perform the same function with armoured vehicles. The tasks for cadets were likely to be the more mundane and routine jobs, such as helping the medically down-graded servicemen, loading and unloading stores, or occasionally helping to hold down a Spitfire which was undergoing ground tests [Fig. 4], or dismantling a Bailey bridge [Fig. 3].

Fig 3. Army Cadets enjoying a snack on a Bailey bridge after a busy morning helping in its erection and dismantling, 1945.

Fig 4. A.T.C. cadets holding down the tail of a Spitfire undergoing standing tests.

Air Cadets from units in Berkshire, including 155 (Maidenhead) Squadron, were employed as pilots' assistants by the Air Transport Auxiliary at White Waltham. The A.T.A. was a civilian ferry organisation which had an advanced flying school at White Waltham. Its purpose was to train pilots to fly twin engine aircraft. They flew Hudson and Albemarle aircraft for this purpose and *'as it was impossible for the pilot* (when flying solo) *to reach all the controls, they employed A.T.C. cadets as pilot's assistants'.*[2]

The Royal Observer Corps was an obvious recruiter of A.T.C. talent. The two organisations used to compete against each other in aircraft recognition competitions, and the young enthusiasts usually acquitted themselves well.

In 1939 the rules for National Service stipulated that youths under 18 *'who can carry messages by motorbike, pedal-cycle or on foot'* could work as part of the Communication Service for the A.R.P.[3] The War Office issued a directive in 1943 explaining the syllabus of training required for cadets undertaking messenger service with the Civil Defence. It stated:

Knowledge of position of control centres, report centres, depots, posts station exchanges and public call boxes in the area in which the messenger will operate.

Art of messenger carrying by written word, orally or by telephone.

Use of local maps with special attention to short cuts and alternative routes for vehicles, cycles or on foot.

Knowledge of the Fire Call system.

Fig 5. Eton College J.T.C. formed a L.D.V. company. Here they are being inspected outside the College gates on 21 June, 1940.

The training for Civil Defence messengers would normally take up to eight hours, and *'cadets so employed will only be required after this initial training for occasional exercises and operational duties'*. The training bore a direct relationship to the Army Cadet War Certificate 'A' syllabus.[4]

The threat of invasion was very real in 1940. The Government, being mindful of what had happened in Holland and Belgium, was worried that enemy troops would be dropped by parachute onto British soil. The Ministry of Information issued a leaflet entitled *If the Invader Comes* ... which listed a set of rules for the civilian population to follow should they find the enemy knocking on their door. The enemy's envisaged airborne assault objective would be to seize control of strategic points such as power stations, aerodromes, telephone exchanges and railway stations. They would either destroy these means of communication or hold them until reinforcements arrived.

In 1860 the Volunteers, forerunner of the Territorial Army, had been formed in response to a supposed threat from the Continent, and cadet units were set up as part of this Volunteer force. The same was to happen in 1940. The Government's response was the formation of the Local Defence Volunteers, a citizens' army. This time however, the cadets were encouraged to join what later became the Home Guard, on an individual rather than a unit basis. Owing to the size and organisation of cadet units, particularly those of the Junior Training Corps in the independent schools, some of their army cadet contingents operated as individual companies within the Home Guard battalion.

Fig 6. A.T.C. Cadet being given instruction on the Tommy gun from a Home Guard Sergeant.

Fig 7. W.J.A.C. girls from Unit 309 [Tooting] receiving skill-at-arms instruction from a Sergeant in the Home Guard, 1944.

Of all the Home Front, war-time-created organisations, the Home Guard was the most involved with the cadet organisations. The Home Guard had a range of personnel, many of whom had seen war service just twenty years previously and had retained their weapon-handling skills. Owing to the practice of call up, and the younger cadet officers and adult NCOs volunteering for military service, the cadets were short of instructors; in many cases this deficiency was made good by volunteer NCOs from the Home Guard. Thus in some parts of the country the Home Guard and the cadet units became reliant on each other; the cadet detachments providing troops and some officers for the Home Guard, whilst the Home Guard, provided instructors.

There was an increasing amount of aerial activity by the enemy during the period 1940 to 1944, particularly in the eastern and southern areas of Britain, which meant that the Home Guard was constantly busy watching for enemy para-troopers. Clearly, the Home Guard could not watch every inch of sky and they relied in part on the assistance and enthusiasm of the cadets in this respect.

The training and operational relationship that the cadet units, and in particular some of the J.T.C. and A.C.F. units had with the Home Guard was integral to their own programme. There is no doubt that the Home Guard at times provided the cadets with an operational responsibility.

The individual cadet's involvement with the Home Guard was evident when a cadet acted as a courier or messenger. It was believed that, should Britain be invaded, messengers would form an important link in the kingdom's defence. A.C.F. Cadet L/Cpl Brown, a messenger for the Home Guard from

Fig 8. Cadet L/Cpl Brown of Ayr Academy ready for Messenger work with the Home Guard, 1942.

99

Cadets and the War, 1939–1945

Fig 9. Army cadets of the 1st/29th A.A. (Searchlight) Cadet Battalion, R.E., undergoing training in unarmed combat by an army P.T. instructor.

Ayrshire, reported in the *Cadet Journal* [1942], saying: *"There are times when a field telephone cannot be used. At such periods the cyclist messenger proves his worth. When the officer in charge is loath to spare a man, as he needs all his trained personnel, he will think of his cyclists"*. Cadet L/Cpl Brown added that the most interesting parts of his work were the night operations. He had been on night manoeuvres with the Home Guard when they assisted the commando troops on training exercises.[5]

There were certain requirements that had to be met by the cadet wanting to operate as a messenger with the Home Guard: first, he had to own a bike as none were issued for cadet use. Secondly, he had to have a good knowledge of the local countryside or town, and thirdly, he had to be a competent map reader – particularly at night.

So prolific was the involvement of the Army Cadets in the work as messengers that the War Office published a training pamphlet titled *Message Writing for Cadets*. Cadets had to learn how to take down messages clearly, and unit commanders had, where necessary, to give the cadets lessons in 'memory practice' and handwriting. Among the skills the cadet messenger had to learn was the use of military abbreviations, and method of describing positions, places and areas. They also had to learn how to use the Royal Signals Messenger Form, AFC2136.

It was not only the country-based units which had a need for despatch riders, urban Home Guard units also required them. Members of the Princess Louise's Kensington Regt., Cadet Corps in London, for example, formed a detachment of 20 cadets to work as 'cyclist despatch riders'. They were attached to the 3rd London Bn. Home Guard and they were specially trained for this work at Sunday morning sessions. On Monday evenings these cadets received additional instruction in unarmed combat to *'prepare them for anything they might be called upon to face should battle in the streets of London come about'*.[6]

In 1942 the age for enrolment in the Home Guard was lowered to 16, with preference for recruitment given to cadets in the Sea Cadet Corps, Junior Training Corps, Army Cadet

100

Fig 10. Party of cadets being given instruction in map reading by a 17 year-old Home Guard Corporal, who is himself a cadet.

Force and the Air Training Corps. This was stated in the War Office (Army Cadet Force Orders No.3) in 1942. By 1941 cadet units were authorized to be affiliated to Home Guard units. For the Army Cadets the directions were more categorical, stating that *'It is the business of every cadet over 17 years of age to join the Home Guard'*, and cadet units were, where possible, to affiliate with the local Home Guard unit. Cadets between the ages of 16 and 17 who were required for anti-aircraft units were confined to specific tasks; those under 17 years of age had to have written consent from their parents or guardian.[7]

Fig 11. Grenade throwing practise for army cadets under the supervision of the Home Guard.

Fig 12. Demonstration of bayonet fighting by Home Guard instructors, for Army Cadets.

Cadets who volunteered for the Home Guard were in most respects to be treated equally with their adult colleagues – except with regard to compensation for loss of earnings and *'disablement attributable to Home Guard service'*. In respect of the former, the rate for boys was less than that for adults, although in the event of an "Action Stations" call out they could be compensated with an extra 1s 6d a day. In the event of disablement, boys of 16 but below 17 would receive half the normal rate of monetary compensation; on attaining the age of 17 years the normal rates applied.[8]

The War Office recognised that Cadet Force officers were already taking command and training young men in military skills. In many cases,

Fig 13. Cadet with Home Guard Sergeant – they are father and son.

Fig 14 War Office training pamphlets for Section Leading and Fieldcraft were exactly the same for the Home Guard, the J.T.C. and A.C.F. cadets.

Fig 15. Captain W. Parry, ex-regular officer and First World War veteran, inspects Army Cadets in 1942. Due to the rapid expansion of the A.C.F. and given his military experience, he was quickly promoted to Lieutenant Colonel and became the first Commandant of Cheshire A.C.F.

therefore, they were encouraged to take command of a Home Guard unit, or act as liaison officers to the local volunteer defence detachment.

The immediate advantage to the Army Cadets in particular was the extension of the cadet training programme. Dual-members who were NCOs could and did introduce cadets to more advanced equipment and activities. It also meant that the transition from the Army Cadets to the Home Guard was smoother and it became the next and most obvious step before progressing to service with the Army.

The dual-commission held by officers commanding the Home Guard and cadet units, and the increasing number of cadets serving with both organisations, meant that a good rapport was maintained. This inter-relationship was further cemented when Major-General The Viscount Bridgeman KBE, CB, DSO, MC became Director of both the Home Guard and the Army Cadet Force.

An invading force would no doubt attempt to command or destroy the country's main means of transportation which at the time was the railways. There was 20,000 miles of rail track in the UK and, despite the independent rail companies forming their own Home Guard units, they could not possibly protect or patrol the whole system. Thus cadet Home Guard contingents assisted in the task. The defence of Shrewsbury Station was partly the responsibility of 'Z' Company of Shrewsbury School cadets. The cadet company shared the responsibility with the other Home Guard companies by being part of a rota system. The J.T.C. cadet contingent, with four other Home Guard companies, undertook six-hour night shifts, one section of the company being on duty from 2230 to 0130 and a second from 0130 to 0430.

Cadets and the War, 1939–1945

The officer commanding 'Z' company drew up a detailed plan of the station area, which included an analysis of the vulnerable points, which stretched over a mile. He concluded that it was impossible to defend the whole area and therefore posted sentries at vital points. There was also a mobile patrol. Sentries were armed with rifles and fixed bayonets. They were to challenge all unauthorised persons by shouting 'HALT'. If the person challenged was unable to give a satisfactory explanation he was to be detained and the police to be notified. It was stipulated, no doubt to the annoyance of the railway employees, that any *'trainman using unauthorised routes ... must be directed to the proper route'.*[9] Thus the defence of Shrewsbury Station was at times in the hands of teenage cadets!

The Home Guard patrolled and observed all means of transportation and communication, including the inland waterways. One of the earliest and perhaps the most organised, was the Upper Thames Patrol (U.T.P.). Within a few days of the Government's call for home defence volunteers, the Tory MP for Abingdon, Sir Ralph Glyn, gained permission to form a waterborne unit to patrol the upper reaches of the Thames. The purpose was to watch over locks, weirs, bridges and pumping stations. Each unit was responsible for a sixteen-mile stretch of the river.[10]

Michael Brooks, a senior pupil and cadet at Radley College, Abingdon, recalls that *'... the Radley Unit of the UTP was responsible for patrolling the Thames from Sandford Lock down to the main line railway bridge above Abingdon'*. The Radley Patrol HQ was the College boat-house. The actual patrol was carried out using the College slipper launch *Lusimus*, for which, it is reported, a special ration of fuel was provided.[11]

Fig 16. Sedbergh Home Guard which had many schoolboy members. In 1940 Sedbergh School formed its own Home Guard company, eventually reaching 100 in total. There was a detailed mobilisation plan and in the event of an emergency the school Home Guard was to guard the Settle to Carlisle Railway. Two operational call-outs occurred; one in 1940 in reaction to an I.R.A. threat, and a second in 1944 when it was feared that the Germans might attempt diversionary parachute raids.

104

The likelihood of an eventual Allied victory put paid to the continuing need for the Home Guard, and the defence force was disbanded in 1944. The War Office urged all 'retirees' to hand in their uniforms to the local Army Cadet unit. So presumably the cadet units got back the Bren guns and other weaponry they had handed over to the Home Guard earlier in the war, following the withdrawal from Dunkirk and the loss of weapons on the beaches of France.

Naturally it was the J.T.C. – which was predominantly army – and the A.C.F. that were involved most with the Home Guard. The other cadet organisations also participated, although to a lesser extent. The A.T.C. enjoyed acting as enemy pilots on exercises with the Home Guard and if there was any waterborne activity the cadets of the Sea Cadet Corps were keen to make themselves available.

It is difficult to assess fully the value of the relationship and assistance the Home Guard rendered the Cadet Movement in general and the J.T.C. and A.C.F. in particular. Instructors, premises, office accommodation, arms and ammunition were loaned – some 'behind the counter'. The arrangement was reciprocal as the cadets provided the Home Guard with added numbers, and in many cases leadership, as when officers held dual commissions. The Home Guard input certainly gave the cadet training added impetus and interest, and provided more advanced and realistic training for the cadets. The liaison between the two military organisations was a close and in many instances a dependent one; indeed, the cadets were often referred to as the Junior Home Guard by the press. The 1st Cadet Battalion The Cheshire Regiment exemplified the close co-operation and the A.C.F. officers actively prepared their cadets for service with the Home Guard by providing more special-ized training for *'those who are approaching the age when they can join the Home Guard'*.[12] The first non-school Cadet Corps, formed in 1940 in Cardiff, used the Home Guard in their recruiting drive by advertising in the local paper asking, *'what a lad could do who was too young to join the Home Guard (then L.D.V.) but who could use a rifle'*. The result was fifty-eight new recruits turning up and 'signing on' the following parade night.[13] The Cardiff Cadet Corps was affiliated to the Home Guard and gave the latter every assistance. Members of the Corps received glowing reports whenever they acted as signallers, messengers, orderlies, umpires' orderlies and enemy when the Home Guard was on exercise; the cadets even com-peted against the Home Guard members in rifle shooting matches, and by all accounts the cadets acquitted themselves well.[14]

How many of the 1,200 Home Guards who were killed in the line of duty were also cadets, we will

Fig 17. Cotswold Sea Cadet Corps on river patrol.

Cadets and the War, 1939–1945

probably never know. Nevertheless, those boys who served with the Home Guard rendered the country an inestimable service. Serving as part of the Home Guard or with the other Civil Defence organisations must have given the young cadet participants a real sense of involvement in the country's defence. It ensured that the Cadet Movement felt that their officers, NCOs and many of their more senior cadets were making a real contribution to the war effort in a meaningful military sense. This is a point hitherto unrecognised by those who have written about the Home Guard.

CHAPTER 8

SERVICE WITH THE HOME GUARD

ILLUSTRATIONS

Fig 1.   Sandbags filled by the boys and staff of Birkenhead School are stacked against the buildings as a means of protection against damage by air-raids. Birkenhead School archives.

Fig 2.   A.T.C. Cadets refuelling a bomber.
Gp. Capt R J D Wilcox RAF and A. M. Waddington in *Golden Jubilee for Air Cadets*, 1991.

Fig 3.   Army Cadets enjoying a snack on a Bailey bridge following a busy morning helping in its erection and dismantling, 1945.
Army Cadet Journal, 1945.

Fig 4.   A.T.C. Cadets holding down the tail of a Spitfire undergoing tests. Imperial War Museum, Ref. CH9566.

Fig 5.   Eton College J.T.C. formed a LDV company. Here they are being inspected outside the College gates on 21 June, 1940. Imperial War Museum.

Fig 6.   A.T.C. Cadet receiving instruction on the Tommy gun from a Home Guard Sergeant.
Air Training Corps Gazette, 1941.

Fig 7.   W.J.A.C. cadets from Unit 309 (Tooting) unit receiving skill-at-arms instrcution from a Sergeant in the Home Guard, 1944.
Girls Venture Corps Air Cadets archives.

Fig 8.   Cadet L/Cpl Brown of Ayr Academy ready for messenger work with the Home Guard, 1942.
Army Cadet Journal, 1942.

Fig 9.   Army Cadets of the 1st/29th A.A. (Searchlight) Cadet Battalion, R.E., under going training in unarmed combat by an army P.T. instructor.
Army Cadet Journal, 1942.

Fig 10.   A party of cadets being given instruction in map reading by a 17 year-old Home Guard Corporal, who is himself a cadet. Imperial War Museum, Ref. H11237.

Fig 11.   Grenade throwing practise for army cadets under the supervision of the Home Guard.
Milestones and Memories (Hillside Publishing Co, 1950).

Cadets and the War, 1939–1945

Fig 12.   Demonstration of bayonet fighting by Home Guard instrcutors, for Army Cadets.
Imperial War Museum, Ref. H9760.

Fig 13.   Cadet with Home Guard Staff Sergeant – they are father and son.
Imperial War Museum, Ref. H11239.

Fig 14.   War Office training pamphlets for Section Leading and Fieldcraft were exactly the same for the Home Guard, the J.T.C. and A.C.F. cadets.
W.O. Section Leading and Fieldcraft, 1945.

Fig 15.   Captain W. Parry, ex-regular officer and First World War veteran, inspects Army Cadets in 1942. Due to the rapid expansion of the A.C.F. and given his military experience, he was quickly promoted to Lieutenant Colonel and became the first Commandant of Cheshire A.C.F.
Imperial War Museum, Ref. H22304.

Fig 16.   Sedbergh Home Guard which had many schoolboy members. In 1940 Sedbergh School formed its own Home Guard company, eventually reaching 100 in total. There was a detailed mobilisation plan and in the event of an emergency the school Home Guard was to guard the Settle to Carlisle Railway. Two operational call-outs occurred; one in 1940 in reaction to an IRA threat, and a second in 1944 when it was feared that the Germans might attempt diversionary parachute raids.
Sedbergh School archives, c.1941.

Fig 17.   Cotswold Sea Cadets on river patrol.
Sea Cadet Journal, 1942.

CHAPTER NINE

CONTRIBUTION AND RECOGNITION

Every cadet wanted to feel that he was a part of the military and to believe that he was contributing to the defence of the country. He wanted to engage in training and activities that, where possible, mirrored what the Armed forces were doing. To the air-minded cadet, that meant getting airborne. The R.A.F. did its best to make the cadets' training more interesting and challenging, by giving the aspiring pilots and navigators of the future air-experience flights. Apart from the motivation factor, the air-experience flights served two additionally important purposes. First, they gave cadets some insight into the workings of

Fig 1. An air experience flight for A.T.C. cadets in a DH86 passenger aircraft.

the R.A.F. and the Fleet Air Arm. Secondly, and equally important, they gave the cadet the chance to find out if he actually liked flying.

Sometimes the reality of war-time service was not what was expected. An ex-A.T.C. bandsman recalled visits to R.A.F. Church Fenton in Yorkshire, where he spent time marching to and from the local cemetery as part of cortèges for military funerals to bury dead air crew, most of whom were air gunners – a disconcerting experience. He was, for different reasons, unimpressed with the work of the ground staff as the workshop activities appeared boring and did not fit in with the glamorous image many boys had of the R.A.F.[1]

The work done by the military may at times have seemed tedious but that did not understandably make it less necessary or less dangerous. Organisations that deal with explosives and weapons require a high standard of safety, but accidents do happen. During the war more ordnance was dealt with and doubtless greater risks were taken.

In addition to the twelve-hundred Home Guard personnel who gave their lives, a further 557 were injured. And as mentioned earlier, there is no way of knowing how many of the fatalities or those injured were cadets. Interestingly the War Office insisted that any 16

Cadets and the War, 1939–1945

Fig 2. Headstone of A.T.C. Cadet Geoffrey Stapleton (271 Sqn) Colwyn Bay, who died in 1943, aged 18. He and Cadet Foulkes and the crew of an Avro Anson perished when the airplane disintegrated on a night flying test from R.A.F. Llandwrog.

year-old who was injured while serving with the Home Guard must remain on the books until he had reached the age of 17, and that no compensation would be forthcoming until the individual did reach that age.

Incidents involving aircraft were logged and therefore any injuries or deaths sustained by A.T.C. cadets were recorded. There were thirty-five known accidents logged involving cadets during the years 1942 to 1945. In 1944 No. 966 (Wallingford) Squadron suffered a tragedy when two of its cadets were killed in a Wellington Bomber flying from R.A.F Wallingford; their names are inscribed on the local war memorial.[2] Another fatality involved a German aircraft. This occurred in 1945 when an R.A.F. truck carrying cadets home from a boxing match was strafed by a Messerschmitt: one cadet died from a shrapnel ricochet which hit him in the chest. The highest loss of life occurred on 8 September, 1943 when three cadets from 1180 (Buxton) Squadron were on a cross-country flight in a Lancaster. The aircraft crashed two miles south-east of Wymeswold airfield. A further three cadets were killed in an R.A.F. truck as a result of a road accident.[3]

The names of four more A.T.C. cadets are engraved on the R.A.F. Memorial at Runnymede in Berkshire. Most of the A.T.C. deaths occurred as a result of aircraft breaking up in flight and crashing into the ground or into the sea. No doubt the pressures of war-time with the demand for the quick turnabout of aircraft did, at times, have a devastatingly detrimental effect. In total over fifty air cadets are known to have lost their lives while flying in R.A.F. aircraft.

Fig 3. Guard of Honour for A.T.C. Cadet P.G. Rolfe. He was one of several cadets in an R.A.F. lorry returning from a boxing match at R.A.F. Bircham Newton which was strafed by the Luftwaffe. Cadet Rolfe died from shrapnel wounds on 15 March, 1945.

Fig 4. Lowestoft A.T.C. cadets on Reedham Marshes recovering part of a Liberator Bomber in 1944.

Apart from flying cadets in aircraft, some A.T.C. units were called upon to assist the Home Guard during their training manoeuvres by acting either as crashed pilots or as enemy airmen; no doubt those cadets asked to do the latter enjoyed the escape and evasion exercises. Cadets were sometimes drafted in to help find, and recover parts of crashed aircraft.

Interestingly, the Sea Cadet Corps made provision for the injured amongst its ranks. As early as 1936 the Sun Hill Court Convalescent Home, which accommodated 30 boys, was established at Worthing. The Naval Service authorities and the Ministry of Health granted free medical treatment for members of the S.C.C. By 1945 it was agreed that any treatment for an injury sustained during training should be given to a conclusion and not merely, as formerly, until the patient was able to travel home. The arrangement also applied to officers, adult C.P.O. instructors and enrolled civilian instructors as well as cadets. The other cadet organisations had no such amenity.[4]

To those living in the more remote parts of the countryside, the danger was, in the main, limited to accidents while training. The risks of travelling in an R.A.F. aircraft apart, by far the greatest threat to people at home was aerial bombing. To those living near the docks and industrial areas of London, Liverpool, Glasgow, Coventry, Southampton, Bristol, Swansea and any other large industrial city, the possibility of devastation from aerial bombing was very real. And those towns on the Eastern side of the country and in the flight path of enemy bombing runs, were always vulnerable to sustaining damage from the air.

In August 1939, London experienced its first 'blackout'; the purpose of which was to avoid providing enemy aircraft with navigational assistance at night and equally importantly to deny them target recognition. The blackout restrictions applied to streets, factories and homes. Later, vehicle lights had to be masked, which resulted in an increase in traffic accidents with many more pedestrians being killed. It also made attendance at parade nights for cadets somewhat hazardous in some areas; finding one's way to the local cadet HQ and returning home in the dark was not easy, and if caught in an air raid it would have been positively dangerous.

111

Fig 5. The remains of Stepney Army Cadet Force headquarters in London following an air attack.

The larger cities and ports took the brunt of the blitz bombardments. The first mass raids began over London on 7th September 1940 and this included London's East End and Docklands which caused over 2,000 casualties. Fatalities from V2 rocket attacks reached a peak of 250 a week in England in 1944. In some cases, cadet headquarters were

Fig 6. The damage done to Stepney A.C.F. H.Q. by a V2 rocket in 1944. Cadets can be seen trying to salvage something from the debris.

Fig 7. Beckenham S.C.C. headquarters after an air raid in 1944.

completely destroyed, whereupon there were desperate attempts to find alternative accommodation large enough to house a cadet unit, many of which were over a hundred strong.

All cadets, particularly during the war, had increased opportunities to put their training to full use, to demonstrate resourcefulness and possibly to perform courageous acts that went beyond the call of duty.

In recognition, and as if in anticipation of the forthcoming war the Navy League in 1938 instituted the Navy League Cross 'For Gallantry'. Before the onset of war only two cadets had been awarded the medal. By 1943 it had gone to a further 12 cadets. Initially most of the awards were for rescuing young boys and children from drowning, but in 1941 Cadet Petty officers A. Howes and S. Nicholson from Hull rescued a soldier, an elderly woman and her two children from a collapsed building following an air raid. In May, 1941

Fig 8 The Navy League Cross for Gallantry.

Sea Cadet H. Thompson of the St. Clement Danes Unit helped to save a block of five shops in the Walworth area of London by making three journeys through falling debris to fetch the fire brigade.[5]

In 1945, 14-year-old Sea Cadet Brian Emery of the Newcastle (Jellicoe) Unit rescued two children who had fallen into the sea from the pier at Cullercoats; for this act of bravery he was rewarded with a Navy League Medal. And Cadet K. Seavers of York, who rescued a Canadian soldier from the River Ouse, was awarded the Navy League Gallantry Cross. The awards were not confined to acts of courage performed during or as a result of air raids, but the latter provided regular opportunities for cadets to apply their training in dangerous situations.[6]

The Air Training Corps also had a Gallantry Medal for cadets. One of the first recipients was Cadet Roy Clark of No. 171 (Christchurch) Squadron who, during a daylight-bombing raid in 1940 and despite injuries to himself, continued to render assistance to the official rescue squad. Most of the awards were for action during air raids. Occasionally a cadet's bravery went far beyond the bounds of the Cadet Service's Gallantry Award. In 1942 Cadet Corporal R. McCallum of No. 49F (Greenock) Squadron went to Buckingham Palace to receive the British Empire Medal (BEM) from the King. His action involved carrying messages by bicycle while bombs and debris were falling. A second Air Cadet recipient of the BEM was Corporal B. Gill of No. 220 (Torquay) Squadron who, while acting as a messenger for the Civil Defence rescued, along with a British and an American serviceman, two victims from a bombed basement whilst running the risk of being blown up by escaping gas. A third Air Cadet L. Wells from No. 244

Cadets and the War, 1939–1945

Fig 9. A.C.F. Corporal D Lazarus, the only cadet recipient of the George Medal.

(Scafell) Squadron rescued a pilot from a crashed burning aircraft; he also was awarded the BEM.[7]

The Army Cadet Force had no such system of gallantry medals, although there were certificates presented to cadets who performed outstanding acts of bravery. In 1941 one of the highest civilian awards was presented to Army Cadet Corporal David Lazarus; it was the George Medal. The award was announced in the *London Gazette*. The citation read:

During an air raid on London Volunteer Lazarus, aged 17 was on his way to report for duty when a bomb fell on a block of tenement flats. The building was reduced to ruins. Masonry and other debris was falling continuously, but Lazarus entered the ruins and began to remove quantities of wreckage with his hands in order to get to four people who were imprisoned. He managed to bring them out, despite the fact that he had already sustained injury himself. He then attempted to rescue a fifth occupant of the flats, but a wall collapsed and buried him. He was taken to hospital suffering from multiple injuries to the head, arms and body.[8]

There are several accounts of cadets from each of the Services helping in the rescue of people trapped in bombed-out buildings, and there is no doubt that numerous acts of courage displayed by members of the Cadet movement remain unknown and unrecognised to this day.

Most cadets entered the Armed Services on reaching the age of 17¾, except for those who, to their undoubted disappointment were compelled to do their national service down the coal mines – they were known as the 'Bevin Boys' after the Minister of Labour, Ernest Bevin. Service down the mines for ex-cadets who longed to serve in the military was a source of discontent. Mr. Ernest Bevin, responded, in 1943, to the plea by cadets who wanted to go to the Service of their choice, by saying:

In the interest of fairness as between individuals the exclusion from the ballot will be limited to three classes ... who ... must be kept for other duties. They are: (1) men accepted for flying duties in the R.A.F. or Fleet Air Arm; (2) men accepted as artificers in submarines; and (3) men in a short list of highly skilled occupations and (who) are not even called up for coal mining.

Thus, Air and Sea Cadets who had been attested – assessed – and were earmarked for flying or work in submarines were exempt from working in the coal mines. It was pointed out by an Army recruiting officer that selection for the mines, under the National Service Act, did not occur until a boy was about 17 years of age, and therefore the Army Cadets could volunteer for the Army at the age of seventeen – provided they had their parents' consent – and thus avoid the coal mines.[9] How many cadets either opted for or were coerced into joining the Army earlier than they might normally have chosen to do, is not known. Suffice it to say, that ex-cadets who became miners could not use the military training they had received, and, of course, there were no medals and no outward recognition for their contribution to the war effort, although they were paid more than the basic military wage.

The R.A.F. air-experience flights and re-designed training pamphlets; the Royal Navy's Bounty Scheme and the 'Y' Scheme; the Army's re-designed Cadet War Certificate and the experiments in airborne and 'town fighting', and all-Arms insistence on technical training, are evidence of the importance to the Armed Forces, and therefore the country, of the Pre-Service Cadet Organisations and the training they provided.

Over 80,000 boys left the cadet units each year to join the Armed Forces; 40,000 of whom went into the Army and the same number into the R.A.F., although the latter's need to recruit had decreased significantly by 1944.[10] Cadet contribution to the war effort cannot be measured in numbers alone nor was it confined to the training and preparation of future combatants. Many cadets experienced Operations at home as part of the Home Guard, and those cadets who held dual membership of the Home Guard and were part of the anti-aircraft artillery batteries experienced active service; others became involved with the Observer Corps, the Civil Defence and the A.R.P.

Cadets who were also members of the Home Guard were unlikely to serve the three years necessary to qualify for the Defence Medal as they would have been called-up for service with the regular forces. The public school masters who served with the Junior Training Corps had T.A. commissions and were eligible for the Territorial Decoration Medal, but officers of the S.C.C., A.C.F. and A.T.C. were not – unless they already held a Reserve Forces-type commission. The imbalance was partly redressed in 1942 when the officers of the A.C.F. and the A.T.C. were granted the King's Commission in recognition of the valuable war work they did. The anomaly regarding recognition of service was eradicated in 1948 when the J.T.C. was re-named the Combined Cadet Force and put on the same footing as the other cadet organisations. Finally in 1950, a long-service Cadet Forces Medal was instituted for all cadet officers and adult NCOs, partly in recognition of the work they did during the Second World War.[11]

Further proof, if any were needed that the contribution the Cadet Movement made towards the war effort was significant and recognised, came at the most public level when H.M. the King became Admiral of the Sea Cadet Corps, Colonel in Chief of the Army Cadet Force and Commodore of the Air Training Corps.

As expected, numbers in the Cadet Movement decreased once the emergency of war was over. Evacuees returned home and some countryside detachments, thus depleted in membership, closed. R.A.F. recruitment ceased in 1944 and Air Training Corps numbers fell to 170,000; by 1946 this was further reduced to 57,000. The Army Cadet Force was reduced to 100,000, although the school-bound Junior Training Corps remained at 30,000.[12] The Sea Cadet Corps' membership was halved and by 1947 was down to 22,000.[13]

There was talk of amalgamating the cadet organisations and forming a single United Services Training Corps. The subject was raised in the House of Commons and the House of Lords. There were three concerns, said the Duke of Montrose who wanted to know *'what steps had been taken to co-ordinate Pre-Service cadet training? Secondly, was it intended that they should be recognised and financially aided after the war? And thirdly, what was to be their relation to the organization of youth as a whole?'* It was decided that they should continue to be under the control of the Inter-Services Cadet Committee rather than, as suggested by some, the Board of Education; thus they continued to receive military assistance and 'sponsorship'. Major-General the Viscount Bridgeman, who had been in charge of the Army Cadets during the war, stated that those who talked about co-operation would *'do well to remember that the Cadet Forces exist for the benefit of the Services to which they belong'.*[13] And Mr. Clement Attlee, the Deputy Prime Minister pointed out that if the proposal for amalgamation was adopted, *'the whole purpose and objective which had inspired members of the organisation would be lost'.* His answer to the proposal for integration was therefore a definite 'No'.[14]

The country was no longer on a war footing and so cadet training, although military based, had to be concerned with more than just the attainment of military aims. The Government voiced what the S.C.C. and A.T.C., via their civilian welfare committees, had always practised: namely, the involvement of the community in the life of the cadet unit, as well as the interests of the parent Service.[15] The A.C.F. was wary of what happened at the end of the First World War when the Territorial Cadet Force of that time was wholly committed to military training. In 1918 people generally were so devastated by the enormity of the first universal conflict and the horrendous casualty list, that their interest in military service decreased sharply and cadet units closed as a result. At the time, the majority of the T.A. Commandants had ignored the cadets' future and were not interested in providing any support for the Army Cadet Force, so the organisation suffered the ignominy of closing down in the 1920s, albeit temporarily. It was however, kept going unofficially in a much truncated form by a group of senior officers until it was re-instated after a hiatus lasting two years.[16]

Wednesday, 19th September
MERCHANT NAVY DAY. Ceremony in Trafalgar Square at 12.15 p.m. Display on the Thames from 12 noon to 7 p.m.

Thursday, 20th September
BRITISH EMPIRE DAY. Ceremony in Trafalgar Square, commencing at 12.15 p.m.

Friday, 21st September
RECONSTRUCTION DAY. Ceremony in Trafalgar Square, commencing at 12.15 p.m. *Speaker*: The Right Hon. George Tomlinson, M.P.

Saturday, 22nd September
"YOUTH AND THE FUTURE" DAY. Ceremony in Trafalgar Square at 12.15 p.m. *Speakers*: Group Captain Bader and Miss Jean Batten.
There will be a DISPLAY by Units of the pre-Service Cadet Corps and of National Youth Organisations at the "Cockpit," Hyde Park, commencing at 3 p.m.

Visit The
VICTORY OVER JAPAN
and
AIRCRAFT EXHIBITIONS
both in Oxford Street, and
DISPLAY
OF CAPTURED AIRCRAFT
Hyde Park, near Marble Arch.
ALL FREE !
SAVE Cost You Nothing !
Gives You Something !
Victor, London.

Fig 10. "Youth and The Future Day" – a printed public announcement for week of events in September, 1945.

Fig 11. Cadets from the three branches of the Armed Forces were always in demand for public parades and at the end of the war they, along with all other wartime organisations, joined in the celebratory parades.

As a result of the change in emphasis, with the cadets' military training being geared to the development of the individual as a useful member of society rather than just the production of a future soldier, sailor or airman, the phrase 'citizenship training' became a cornerstone of all cadet training. The new thinking as regards the Cadet Movement was also in keeping with the Youth Advisory Council's philosophy outlined in the report entitled The Purpose and Content of the Youth Service.[17] The leadership courses and training which cadets underwent were seen as a benefit regardless of their chosen career.

At the same time, two of the branches of the Cadet Movement and their parent Armed Services wanted to ensure that the close links forged during the war would be maintained. The A.C.F. was actively seeking T.A. officers and instructors with recent military experience whilst the A.T.C. was pleased to become part of the R.A.F. Reserve Command. The Sea

Cadets and the War, 1939–1945

Cadet Corps, on the other hand, preferred to adopt a more independent approach and were mainly under the direction of the Navy League. Nevertheless, the basic military skills gained by cadets would still prove to be useful as conscription, via National Service for all eighteen-year-old youths was to continue for another seventeen years.

The joint aims of military efficiency and good citizenship were clearly stated in 1944 by General Sir Bernard L. Montgomery, KCB, DSO, writing in *The Cadet Journal*. (Fig. 12)

In 1945 the church bells were rung again. Parades and exhibitions were held. Britain justifiably celebrated the end of six years of hostility. And everyone, especially those in uniform, (including the Pre-Service Cadet Organisations and the National Girls Training

Message to the Army Cadet Force

from

General Sir Bernard L. Montgomery, KCB, DSO.

When I visited the Army Cadet Force Exhibition in London I was impressed with the enthusiasm which I saw among the members of the Force at the Exhibition. I am sure this same enthusiasm inspires the Cadet Force throughout the Country.

Do not allow this enthusiasm to flag; do not allow other interests to divert you from the objective which you have set before you - that of becoming efficent soldiers and good citizens. In the coming months the Army will need every man who can be spared from other work and we shall look to members of the Army Cadet Force to be with us at the finish. You will find that the training which you have received as cadets will increase your value to the Army and the Country and will help to bring nearer the day of victory.

With God's help the end is not far off. This is the moment when every man and boy in the country must turn with renewed vigour to the job on hand.

Fig 12. Message from General Sir Bernard L Montgomery KCB, DSO, 1944.

Corps) took the opportunity to mark the occasion in the best way they could. The A.T.C. planned a rally to be centred on the England v Scotland football match at the Tottenham Hotspur ground. This happily coincided with the end of the war in Europe and it became a Victory celebration. Two thousand A.T.C. cadets descended on London for a parade in Hyde Park. All the cadets were accommodated in an underground shelter in Camden Town tube station, which was fitted out with three-tier beds for the occasion.[18] The Sea Cadets combined with the Royal Navy as part of the 'Victory at Sea' exhibition held in London; the aim was to raise money for the Sea Cadets' Navy League Fund. The week from 15th–22nd September 1945 was designated by the Government as 'Thanksgiving Week' and church services, and parades were held in London, culminating in a 'Youth and Future Day'. There was a march-past of Pre-service Cadet Corps and National Youth Organisations in Hyde Park. In the following year, 1946, there was another parade in Hyde Park. On this occasion, it involved only the Army Cadet Force, and 6,000 army cadets from the UK and Northern Ireland marched past Her Royal Highness Princess Elizabeth, the future Queen.

It is true to say that at the end of hostilities, all cadets felt that they had made some worthwhile contribution to the war effort, and at the same time had learnt a great deal. No doubt, many had some excitement also. Nevertheless, some lost their headquarters in air-raids; some were decorated while still cadets and some even lost their lives. Over half a million male and female cadets either volunteered or were conscripted for service with the Armed Services and many volunteered for part-time duty with other uniformed organisations. This contribution as already noted has hitherto received hardly any recognition. It is hoped therefore that this book will have put into place a small piece of the military historical puzzle, whilst at the same time paying tribute to those young people who felt duty bound to play their part and don cadet uniform during the years 1939–45 when Britain was at war.

CHAPTER 9

CONTRIBUTION AND RECOGNITION

ILLUSTRATIONS

REFERENCES

Chapter One   *RECRUITMENT AND EXPANSION*

1. L. J. Collins. *CADETS – The Impact of War on the Cadet Movement* [Jade Publishing Ltd., 2001] p. 63.

2. Boyle, Brian [Ed]. *The Who's Who of Children's Literature* [Evelyn Hughes, London, 1968] p. 159.

Chapter Two   *GETTING FIT TO SERVE*

1. Brigadier Wand-Tetley CBE, 'Physical Fitness in the A.C.F.' in *The Cadet Review*, 1945.

2. War Office, Pre-Service Physical Training and Recreation for Army Cadets [HMSO, 1943].

3. War Office, Physical Efficiency Preparation for Service Cadets [HMSO, 1945].

4. 'Air-Borne Training'
   Army Cadet Journal, 1945.

Chapter Three   *THE DEMAND FOR TECHNICAL TRAINING*

1. War Office, Technical Training in the Army Cadet Force [War Office, 1945].

2. 'The Bounty Scheme' *The Navy League Journal*, 1941.

3. 'H.M.S. Foudroyant' *The Navy League Journal*, 1945.

4. 'War Office, Technical Training' *Army Cadet Journal*, 1943.

5. C/Capt. Andrews and Capt C. Midgley, *Army Cadet Proficiency* [Wheaton, Exeter, 1943] pp. 56-59.

6. ibid p. 60.

7. C. P Rawson and S. G Saunders, *The Air Cadets Handbook of English* [Allen & Unwin, 1943].

8. Air Ministry, *Air Training Corps Rules and Regulations* [Air Ministry, 1941].

9. The Navy League, *SHIP'S COMPANY – A Handbook for The Sea Cadet Corps* [Gale & Polden, 1945].

10. 'Technical Training in the ACF' *Army Cadet Journal*, 1942.

Cadets and the War, 1939–1945

Chapter Four　　　　　*TRAINING FOR GIRLS*

1.　　The Navy League Sub-Committee Minutes Report 21 May 1942.

2.　　ibid.

3.　　Comments adjoining photograph of W.J.A.C. *Air Training Corps Gazette*, 1942.

4.　　Editorial comment *Army Cadet Journal*, 1942.

5.　　'Pre-Service Units Co-operate' *Air Training Corps Gazette*, 1943.

6.　　'Girls' Training Corps' *Chard & Ilminster News*, April, 1942.

7.　　'Cadet News from All Quarters' *Army Cadet Journal*, 1944.

8.　　'Girls' Training Corps' ibid, 1942.

Chapter Five　　　　　*ON PARADE AND IN THE PUBLIC EYE*

1.　　'Trafalgar Day' *Sea Cadet Corps Journal*, 1945.

2.　　'Wings for Victory' *Chard & Ilminster News*, March 1943.

3.　　'Salute the Soldier Week' *Chard & Ilminster News*, April 1944.

4.　　'A.C.F. Salute the Soldier' *Army Cadet Journal*, 1944.

5.　　Leonard Moseley, *Backs to the Wall – London under Fire, 1940-1945* [London; Weidenfeld, 1971] p 300/1.

6.　　Flying Aces' *Air Training Corps Gazette*, 1942.

Chapter Six　　　　　*BASIC MILITARY TRAINING*

1.　　'Lending Company's rifles to Home Guard' *The Cadet Journal*, 1942.

2.　　School Weapons of War Memories from H L Ross – Birkenhead School Archives.

3.　　'T.S Undaunted' *Sea Cadet Corps Journal*, 1944.

4.　　Lt. Col. H. J. Harris, *Rugby School Corps, 1860-1960* [London, Brown & Truscott, 1960].

5.　　The Navy League – *SHIP'S COMPANY, a handbook for the Sea Cadet Corps.* [Gale & Polden, 1945].

6.　　'Officer Training' *Sea Cadet Corps Journal*, 1943.

7.　　'Officer Training' *Army Cadet Journal*, 1941.

8.   'Appointment of a Director' *Air Training Cadet Gazette*, 1942.

9.   'Combined Service' *Army Cadet Journal*, 1944.

10.   'Youth Leaders' Problems – Conference at Shrewsbury' *The Border Counties Advertiser*, 12 May, 1943.

Chapter Seven   *COURSES AND CAMPS*

1.   Foudroyant and Her History S.C.C. Journal, 1943 and 1944.

2.   'Sea Cadets and the Merchant Navy' *Sea Cadet Corps Journal*, 1944.

3.   'The 'Y' Scheme' *Sea Cadet Corps Journal*, 1943.

4.   'Mechanical Training' *Sea Cadet Corps Journal*, 1943.

5.   L. J. Collins, *CADETS – The Impact of War on the Cadet Movement* [Jade Publishing Ltd., 2001] pp. 73-76.

6.   Wg. Cdr. H. W. Lamond R.A.F. (Retd), *History of the Air Training Corps - including the A.D.C.C. and the C.C.F.* [Unpublished: HQ. A.T.C. R.A.F. Cranwell, 1984] pp. 2-12.

7.   op. cit. L. J. Collins, pp. 153/4.

8.   ibid.

9.   op. cit. L. J. Collins, pp. 142/3.

10.   'Town-fighting' *Army Cadet Journal*, 1944.

Chapter Eight   *SERVICE WITH THE HOME GUARD*

1.   John Stacpoole (Ed), *Sedbergh School 1900 – 2000* [The Old Sedbergian Club, 2000] pp. 71-96.

2.   (Ed) Flt. Lt. K. S. Tipping RAFVR(T), (Retd) *Thames Valley Wing and Its Squadrons.* [Thames Valley Wing ATC, 1991] p. 34.

3.   Army Cadet Force Orders No. 3 [War Office, 1943] pp. 1-4.

4.   H.M.S.O., National Service, 1939, pp. 1-5.

5.   'Messenger with the Home Guard' *Army Cadet Journal*, 1942.

6.   'Messenger Work for the Home Guard' *Army Cadet Journal*, 1942.

7.   op cit. Army Cadet Force Orders No. 3.

8.   ibid.

9.   No. 1 Bn. Home Guard (Shropshire Zone) SECRET Operation Order No. 3, Shrewsbury School Archives, c.1940.

10.   David Caroll, *Dad's Army: The Home Front, 1939-45* [Sutton Publishing, UK 2002].

11.   ibid.

12.   '1st Cadet Battalion The Cheshire Regiment' *Army Cadet Journal*, 1941.

13.   '1st Cardiff non-school Cadet Corps' *Army Cadet Journal*, 1942.

Chapter Nine   *CONTRIBUTION AND RECOGNITION*

1.   Letter from Mr Mike Waddington ex-A.T.C. cadet, 1997.

2.   (Ed) Flt. Lt. K. S. Tipping RAFVR(T) (Retd) *Thames Valley Wing and Its Squadrons* [Thames Valley Wing A.T.C., 1991] p. 47.

3.   *Air Cadet Review*, No 4, 1992.

4.   'Sun Hill Court' *Sea Cadet Corps Journal*, 1945.

5.   'Gallantry Award' *Sea Cadet Corps Journal*, 1942

6.   ibid.

7.   Wg. Cdr. H. W. Lamond R.A.F. (Retd), *History of the Air Training Corps – including the A.D.C.C. and the C.C.F. (R.A.F.)* [Unpublished: H.Q. A.T.C., R.A.F. Cranwell, 1984], pp. 3-20.

8.   *London Gazette*, February 1941.

9.   'Cadets as Coal Miners' *Army Cadet Review*, 1945.

10.   Douglas Cooke, M.C. M.A (Gen. Ed), *Youth Organisations of Great Britain, 1944-45* [London: Jordan & Sons, 1944], p. 191 Air Cadet Facts, No. 1, January 1983, AC/2735/PR(ED3) A.C.F.A., *The Official Handbook of the A.C.F.* [London: A.C.F.A., 1949].

11.   L. J. Collins, *CADETS – The Impact of War on the Cadet Movement* [Jade Publishing Ltd., 2001], p. 167-8.

12.   ibid. p 184.

13.   ibid. p 184.

14.   Major-Gen The Viscount Bridgeman C.B., D.S.O., M.C. 'Combined Service' *Army Cadet Journal*, 1944.

15.   'Parliament and the A.C.F.' *Army Cadet Journal*, 1944.

16.   L. J. Collins, op cit. pp 45-60.

17.   Youth Advisory Council, *The Purpose and Content of the Youth Service* H.M.S.O., 1945.

18.   L. J. Collins, op cit. pp. 171-177.

BIBLIOGRAPHY

PERIODICALS

Air Defence Corps Gazette
Air Pictorial
Air Training Corps Gazette
Army Cadet Journal & Gazette
Girls' Venture Corps Air Cadets Magazine
The Cadet Revue
The Navy
The Navy League
The Sea Cadet

REPORTS, REGULATIONS and PAMPHLETS

Andrews, P. E. & Midgley, C. *Army Cadet Proficiency* [Wheaton], 1943.
Atherton, J. G. *Home and Away and Home to Stay, evacuee's diary, 1939-1940*, Imperial War Museum.
A.C.F.A. Instructions for Candidates and Conduct of Certificate 'A' examinations, A.C.F.A. – 9/Cadets/580 (M.T.Ac), 1945.
A.T.C. From A.T.C. to R.A.F. and Fleet Air Arm [Sidders] c.1944.
Air Ministry Order No. A484, 1940.
Air Ministry Air Training Corps Rules and Regulations, 1941.
B.N.A.C. A Handbook for Cadet Officers [Gale & Polden], 1943.
H.M.S.O. Air Raid Precautions Handbook No. 8 (Home Office), 1938.
H.M.S.O. National Service, 1939.
H.M.S.O. The Purpose and Content of the Youth Service (Youth Advisory Council) 1945.
H.M.S.O. The Battle of Britain – An Air Ministry Account c.1941.
H.M.S.O. The Navy and the Y Scheme, 1944 Navy League and S.C.C. Sub-Committee Minutes 1939-45, S.C.C. HQ files, London
HQ Air Cadets *Air Cadets Facts, No.1*, 1983.
Hughes, H.C., TD MA Lt Col. *The Army Cadets of Surrey 1860 – 1960* [London, Owen Spyer] 1960.
M.A.O. 8 (S.C.C.) *History of the Cadet Movement*
Lamond H.W. RAF Wg. Cdr. (Retd) *The History of the Air Training Corps 1938-1983* [HQ. A.T.C. & C.C.F. RAF Cranwell] 1984.
Rawson C.P. and Saunders S.G., *Air Cadet's Handbook of English* [Allen & Unwin], 1943.
Souvenir Pamphlet, *Golden Jubilee' of Air Cadets in the East Essex Wing, 1941-1991* [East Essex Wing A.T.C.] 1991.
Tipping, K. S. Flt. Lt. RAFVR(T), *Thames Valley and Its Squadrons A Short History to Commemorate the Fiftieth Anniversary of the A.T.C.* [Thames Valley Wing A.T.C.] 1991.
The Navy League, *Ship's Company – A Handbook for The Sea Cadet Corps* [Gale & Polden], 1945.
W.O. Pre-Service Physical Training and Recreation for Army Cadets, 1943.
W.O. Message Writing for Cadets, part V. 1945.
W.O. Physical Efficiency Preparation for Pre-Service Cadets, 1945.
W.O. Section Leading and Fieldcraft for Cadets, 1945.
W.O. Technical Training in the Army Cadet Force, 1945.

BOOKS

A.C.F.A. *A Camp Handbook for Officers, NCOs and Cadets* [London: A.C.F.A. 1947].

A.C.F.A. *The Official Handbook of the A.C.F.A.* [London: A.C.F.A. 1949].

A.C.F.A. *The Army Cadet Force Handbook* [London: A.C.F.A. 1955].

A.C.F.A. *The Cadet Story 1860-1960* [London: A.C.F.A. 1982].

Boyle, Brian [Ed]. *The Who's Who of Children's Literature* [Evelyn Hughes: 1968].

Brayley, Martin. *The British Home Front 1939-45* [Osprey: 2005].

Collins, L. J., *CADETS-The Impact of War on the Cadet Movement* [Jade Publishing Ltd., 2001].

Cooke, M.C. and Douglas, M.A. (Eds) *Youth Organisations of Great Britain 1944-45,* [Jordan: 1945].

Devane, Rev. R.S. *Challenge From Youth* [Browne & Nolan: 1942].

Foley, Col. F.W. *A Short History of the Frimley and Camberley Cadet Corps 1908-1948* [Gale & Polden: 1948].

Gawthorn P.R. (Ed), *Empire Youth Annual* [Gawthorn Ltd: 1946].

Harris, Lt Col. *Rugby School Corps 1860-1960* [Brown, Knight & Truscott: 1960].

MacKenzie, J. M., The Home Guard [OUP: 1995].

Marwick, Arthur, *The Home Front – The British and the Second World War* [Macmillan: 1986].

Moseley, L. *Backs to the Wall – London under Fire, 1940-1945* [Weidenfeld: 1971].

Mussett, N.J. *Cadets at Giggleswick 1910-1980* [Giggleswick School: 1980].

Oldham, M.A. and Basil J., *A History of Shrewsbury School 1852-1952* [Blackwell: 1952].

Percival, Alicia, *Youth Will Be Led – the story of the youth organisations* [Collins: 1957].

Philpott, Brian, *Challenge in the Air* [Models & Allied: 1971].

Riley, M.A. *Sherborne in Uniform* [Shelly: 1988].

Sainsbury, Lt. Col. J.D. The *Hertfordshire Yeomanry – an illustrated history 1794-1920* [Hart Books: 1994].

Springall, J. *Youth, Empire and Society* [Croom Helm: 1977].

Cadets and the War, 1939–1945

Stacpoole, J. (Ed). *Sedbergh School 1900-2000* [The Old Sedbergian Club: 2000]

Stock Exchange Cadet Company, Milestones and Memories 1926 – 1950 [Hillside Publishing Co, 1950]

Taylor, Leonard. *The Story of the Air Training Corps* [Air League of the British Empire: 1946]

Trist, Lt. Col. L. H. *A Short History of Rossall School Corps* [*Fleetwood Chronicle*: 1960]

Wells, Capt. J. *The Royal Navy – An Illustrated History 1870-1982* [Sutton: 1994]

INDEX

Cadets and the War, 1939-1945

Cadets and the War, 1939–1945

Cadets and the War, 1939–1945

Trafalgar 1, 41-42, 44, 65, 66

U

U-boat 67
United Services Training Corps 115
United States Air Force 43

V

Victoria Cross 41

W

W.A.A.F. 24, 33
W.J.A.C. 31, 33-36, 39-40, 52, 80, 99
W.J.A.C. Units:
1165 Unit 34
Harrow unit 80
Unit 309 [Tooting] 99
Worthing Unit 33
W.R.E.N.S. 33
Wakefield, Mr W. W., M.P., the Director of the A.T.C. 41
Wand-Tetley, Brigadier 9
War Agricultural Committee 77
War Certificate 'A' 10, 14
War Office xiv, 2, 10, 14, 17, 19, 28, 46, 57, 59, 97, 100-102, 105, 109
War Weapons Week 41
Warship Week 41
Waterborne 26, 27
Waterloo 1
Weapons 1
Bangalore Torpedoes 96
Bren guns 51-52, 77, 105
Field Gun 54
grenade throwing 9, 101
Lee Enfield 51-52
Lewis Machine Gun 55-56
Martini-Henry carbine 52
Mortar 79
Sten sub-machine gun 43, 51-52
Tommy gun 98
V2 rocket 112
Vickers medium machine 77
Wellington 1
Western Command 10

Cadets and the War, 1939–1945